Simple.

The Christian Life
Doesn't Have to
Be Complicated.

Robert J. Morgan

Simple.

The Christian Life Doesn't Have to Be Complicated.

Robert J. Morgan

Randall House Publications
114 Bush Road
PO Box 17306
Nashville, TN 37217 USA
www.RandallHouse.com

Simple. The Christian Life Doesn't Have to Be Complicated.
By Robert J. Morgan
Published by Randall House Publications
114 Bush Road
Nashville, Tennessee 37217

© Copyright 2006
Robert J. Morgan

Printed in the United States of America
ISBN 0892655623
Library of Congress Control Number: 2006926918

contents

Affectionately dedicated
to my granddaughter,

Morgan Cate, who is a
bundle of energy and the apple
of her Poppa's eye.

It's Simple

The Christian life is SIMPLE.

No, not always *easy*, but remember—Christianity doesn't have to be complicated. We tend to make things harder than they are because, after all, life is unimaginably complex, and everything that exists *does* consist of innumerable moving parts. Nor are the complicated answers necessarily wrong. Ask a group of chemists, for example, to describe water. They'll tell you that a water molecule is made up of two hydrogen atoms and one oxygen atom, and it can be split into its constituent elements through electrolysis, causing the water molecules to dissociate into H+ and OH- ions, which are pulled toward the cathode and anode respectively.

Ask a group of children about water, and they'll tell you it's something you drink when you're thirsty. Both answers happen to be correct.

Ask a philosopher or theologian about Christianity and you may get an esoteric answer that may be correct in every respect. But you don't have to be a chemist to enjoy a cool drink of water, nor must you be a canonized saint to enjoy the living water offered by Jesus Christ. The more we study the Bible, of course, the deeper and richer we'll be; but Christianity is best enjoyed simply.

Nearly 200 years ago, America's greatest philosopher, Henry David Thoreau, wrote that to live simply was to live wisely; his basic rule for healthy living was: "Simplify! Simplify!"

If anyone should be an expert in simplicity, it's the Christian. It's not that we're simple-*minded*; we deal with the deepest truths under heaven. But we are simple of heart and habit. And while our beliefs are deep enough to challenge the world's greatest thinkers, they're plain enough for children to understand.

Success in life comes from sticking with the basics of the Bible, the ABCs of the Christian faith, namely:

- Assurance – How can I know for sure?
- Baptism – Why should I get wet?
- Church – What's it got to offer?
- Devotions – How can I stay close to God?
- Evangelism – How can I share my faith with others?

As you read through the next several chapters, please note the additional features. Throughout this book are side-bars for additional thought, and at the end of each chapter are suggested verses to commit to memory. May the Lord bless you with the simplicity of His grace as you read and study and grow in Christ!

Many thanks goes to Ron Hunter, Emily White, and the wonderful Randall House Publications staff for their encouragement and expertise, and to my agent, Chris Ferebee, for his assistance.

Special thanks to my colleague, Steven Pierce, and his creative design team, who developed the concepts behind this series.

a=assurance.

Can we know for sure? Absolutely? With perfect certitude? How can we really know without a shadow of a doubt that we are going to heaven when we die?

Some years ago, a lady in our church said, "Well, I *hope* I'm saved and going to heaven, but I don't think I can really know for sure."

Another man with a troubled past had similar concerns. During a period of discouragement, he relapsed and started drinking again. "I'm not going to heaven now," he said. "I don't think I'm still a Christian."

Another family with a loved one at death's door wanted me to assure them that their dying relative was really going to heaven. "How can we be sure?" they asked. This man was a wonderful Christian, but his family was insecure about his eternal destination.

These are not uncommon experiences. Bill Bright, founder of Campus Crusade for Christ, observed, "My experience in counseling thousands of students and laymen through the years since I met Christ personally has convinced me that there are literally tens of thousands of good, faithful church-goers who have received Christ in prayer, but who are not sure of their salvation."[1]

How different the attitude of the apostle Paul! He exclaimed, "I *know* whom I have believed and am *persuaded* that He is able to keep what I have committed to Him until that Day" (2 Timothy 1:12, emphasis mine).

Elsewhere he wrote, "I am *persuaded* that neither death nor life, nor angels nor principalities nor powers, nor things present nor things to come, nor height nor depth, nor any other created thing, shall be able to separate us from the love of God which is in Christ Jesus our Lord" (Romans 8:38, 39, emphasis mine).

The patriarch Job declared: "I *know* that my Redeemer lives, And He shall stand at last on the earth; And after my skin is destroyed, this I know, That in my flesh I shall see God" (Job 19:25, 26, emphasis mine).

The psalmist David said, "Now I *know* that the Lord saves His anointed" (Psalm 20:6, emphasis mine).

I have three preliminary thoughts about this:

- Assurance of salvation isn't a matter of whether or not we *feel* saved. Dr. R. A. Torrey wrote in his book for new Christians: "We may feel forgiven, or we may not feel forgiven, but that does not matter. It is not a question of what we feel but of what God says."[2]

- It isn't a matter of knowing the exact *time* and *place* of your conversion. Some people are bothered because they don't know precisely when and where they were born again; but though you may not remember the particulars, God does. It's not a question of what we remember, but of what God has done and of what God has told us in His Word. Acts 16:31 says: "Believe on the Lord Jesus Christ, and you *will* be saved" (emphasis mine). There's no "maybe" or "might be" about it. The Bible uses the vocabulary of certainty. If you are actively trusting Christ right now as your Savior, there had to be a point in your past—perhaps in your childhood—when you began. Thank God for it, and don't anguish if you can't remember the exact time or place.

- On the other hand, it is possible to have a false assurance of salvation. Some people who think they're saved and going to heaven are mistaken. Matthew 7:21-23 is a stark passage of Scripture in which Jesus says: "Not everyone who calls me their Lord will get into the kingdom of heaven.

> Only the ones who obey my Father in heaven
> will get in. On the day of Judgment many will
> call me their Lord. They will say, 'We preached
> in your name, and in your name we forced
> out demons and worked many miracles.' But
> I will tell them, 'I will have nothing to do
> with you!'" (CEV).

There are two vitally important questions to ask and answer. First, do you *know* Christ? Second, do you *know that you know* Christ? In other words: Are you saved, and do you have assurance of your salvation?

We can approach this theme from two different passages of Scripture, both written by the apostle John, the man who can reasonably be called our Lord's best friend on earth. He referred to himself as "the disciple whom Jesus loved." He was the one who sat next to Jesus at the Last Supper and to whom Jesus entrusted the care of His mother as He was dying on the cross. John became the last surviving member of the original apostolic band, and according to our best knowledge, he was the only apostle to have died a natural death. In the New Testament, he wrote the gospel of John, the letters of 1, 2, and 3 John, and the book of Revelation.

One of the things I like best about John's writings is his clarity in stating his reason for writing. His gospel and his first epistle are very similar, and both contain purpose statements at the end of their respective books. These two purpose statements answer our two questions: Do I know Christ? Do I know I know Christ?

John's great statement of purpose for his gospel is found near the end of his book, in John 20:30, 31, "And truly Jesus did many other signs in the presences of His disciples, which are not written in this book; but these are written that you may believe that Jesus is the Christ, the Son of God, and that believing you may have life in His name."

Our Salvation Is Centered in Christ

The first thing to notice is that our salvation is centered in Christ. It begins: *And truly Jesus did many other signs in the presence of His disciples, which are not written in this book.* The word *sign* was John's code word for our Lord's miracles. In his gospel, John describes eight different miracles that Jesus performed. Dr. J. Sidlow Baxter called this "the octave of miracles in John's Gospel."

> *The turning of the water into wine (John 2:1-11)*
> *The healing of the nobleman's son (4:46-54)*
> *The curing of the Bethesda paralytic (5:1-9)*
> *The feeding of the five thousand (6:5-13)*
> *The walking over the sea of Galilee (6:19-21)*
> *The giving of sight to the blind man (9:1-7)*
> *The raising of Lazarus from death (11:1-44)*
> *The miraculous draught of fishes (21:1-11)*

"As all musical sound is comprehended in eights or octaves," wrote Baxter, "so John has comprehended the significance of all our Savior's miracles in these eight."[3]

But now, at the end of his book, John avows that these eight miracles were only a sampling of our Lord's miraculous works. In fact, the very last sentence of the gospel of John says, "And there are also many other things which Jesus did, which if they were written one by one, I suppose that even the world itself could not contain the books that would be written. Amen" (John 21:25).

Jesus came as a Miracle-Worker with supernatural power. But exactly who was He? What was the secret of His identity? Who did He claim to be? John goes on to say, "And truly Jesus did many other signs in the presence of His disciples, which are not written in this book; but these are written that you may believe that Jesus is the Christ, the Son of God" (John 20:20).

Notice those three names or titles for our Lord Jesus.

First, He is Jesus. From one perspective, there was nothing unusual about the name *Jesus*. It was a common designation in the biblical world, and many Jewish parents gave their boys this name. It speaks of His humanity, His ordinariness. But it also speaks of His *extra*ordinariness. Jesus is the New Testament version of the Old Testament name *Joshua*, and it comes from two shorter Hebrew words—the name *Jehovah* coupled with the verb *to save*—literally, "Jehovah Saves." That explains the angel's message to Joseph: "You shall call His name Jesus for He shall save His people from their sins" (Matthew 1:21). This name embodies His mission and conveys His purpose.[4]

The whole teaching of the Bible is this: The God who created us is very powerful and very pure, but all of us have brought shame and disgrace upon ourselves. We are all sinners, and sinners cannot inhabit God's presence in eternity. So God Himself became a man—Jesus Christ—born through the womb of a virgin; He Himself was pure, sinless, and perfect.

When He died on the cross, He bore the penalty and punishment for our sins so that in Him we might have forgiveness and eternal life, not on the basis of our own merits, but on the basis of His righteousness, His death on the cross, and His resurrection from the grave. Romans 4:25 says, "He was delivered over to death for our sins and was raised to life for our justification" (NIV). This truth is all that is bound up in His name *Jesus*—Jehovah Saves!

Second, He is the Christ. "These things were written that you may believe that Jesus is the *Christ*." This is the English translation of the Greek work *Christos*, which was the Greek term for the Hebrew word *Messiah*. It literally means *Anointed One*. Long before Jesus was born in Bethlehem, the Old Testament prophets predicted that a Messiah would be sent into the world, anointed by God, to provide the human race with hope, heaven, forgiveness of sin, and everlasting life. Seven centuries before Christ was born, the prophet Isaiah wrote, "The Spirit of the Sovereign LORD is on me, because the LORD *has anointed me* to preach good news to the poor" (Isaiah 61:1, NIV, emphasis mine). He predicted the coming of the Anointed One, the Christ.

Third, Jesus is the Son of God. "These things were written that you may believe that Jesus is the Christ, the *Son of God*." This is a classic title for Jesus, but many people underestimate its meaning because we don't hear those three words—*Son of God*—as they were understood in Bible times. We take them literally, but among the Hebrews it was an idiomatic phrase. They often used *father*-and-*son* terminology not just to convey lineage, but characteristics. To say "son of" was to mean "possessing the distinctives of."

Simple

For example, Genesis 4 describes two brothers, Jabal and Jubal. Jabal became the "father of those who dwell in tents and have livestock" and Jubal became the "father of all those who play the flute." The builders of the Tower of Babel were called "sons of men" because they exhibited the worst of human behavior. Ministerial students in the Old Testament were called "sons of the prophets." In the Gospels, Jesus referred to James and John as "sons of thunder" because of their volatile temper.

When our Lord called Himself the "Son of Man," He was stressing His humanity. He possessed the characteristics of a human being—He was a man. When He called Himself the "Son of God," He was emphasizing His deity, His god-ness. He wasn't saying that He was less than God or a product or prodigy of God. He was claiming to be God Himself!

It was a message His Jewish audience couldn't miss, as the Bible makes clear in John 5:18, "Therefore the Jews sought all the more to kill Him, because He not only broke the Sabbath, but also said that God was His Father, making Himself equal with God."

Several years ago, an article of mine appeared in a Christian magazine and shortly afterward I received a call from a literary agent in New York City. He had seen my article and felt I had promise as a writer. His agency wanted to represent me. He flew to Nashville to meet with me and told me he could market my manuscripts to big publishing firms in New York. There's

> *Jesus is God! O! could I now*
> *But compass earth and sea,*
> *To teach and tell the single truth,*
> *How happy should I be!*
> *O! had I but an angel's voice,*
> *I would proclaim so loud,*
> *Jesus, the good, the beautiful,*
> *Is everlasting God.*
> *(Frederick W. Faber, 1862)*

just one problem, he said. "You have too much about 'Jesus' in your writings. To appeal to a broader audience, you need to talk less about Jesus and more about positive thinking and religion and attitude and spirituality. Use any other words you want to use—just less about Jesus and less about the Bible."

I had no interest in doing that. If I followed his advice, I would no longer have a reason to write. I wouldn't have a message. It's all about Jesus, the Christ, the Son of the Living God. He is God Himself who became a man and who died on the cross for the sins of the world. He is the Resurrected Savior who rose from the dead to give us eternal life.

The most basic fact of Christianity—the deepest core of our message—is, "For God so loved the world that He gave His only begotten Son, that whosoever believeth in Him should not perish, but have everlasting life" (John 3:16, KJV). Our salvation is centered in Jesus.

> *Jesus only,*
> *Jesus ever,*
> *Jesus all in all*
> *we sing,*
> *Savior, Sanctifier,*
> *and Healer,*
> *Glorious Lord and*
> *coming King!*
> *(A. B. Simpson, 1890)*

Our Salvation Is Conveyed Through Scripture

The second part of John's purpose statement in John 20:20 says that our salvation is conveyed through Scripture. "And truly Jesus did many other signs in the presence of His disciples, which are not written in this book; *but these are written that you may believe that Jesus is the Christ, the Son of God*" (emphasis mine).

"These things are written." In the great wisdom of God, He encapsulated everything He wanted us to know within the covers of a book that we can carry in our hands throughout our lives. As I was preparing this chapter, I took a break to rest on our back porch. Looking up into the sky I was surprised to see skywriters at work. I'd read about skywriting, but had never seen it before. There were evidently five airplanes involved, although they were too high to be visible to the naked eye. They were in perfect formation, and they were each emitting white smoke in measured sequences so that letters were formed. Scrolled across the sky was an advertisement for a vacuum cleaner.

It reminded me of a question I had once asked myself. Why did God not write His gospel in the sky? Why did He not write it in human letters in the stars? The answer was obvious. In ten minutes, the vacuum cleaner advertisement, dramatic as it was, had disappeared, blown away with the winds of heaven, the white smoke merging with the clouds and dissipating into the atmosphere as though it had never been there at all. But a literal, physical book—one that can be held in our hands and opened on our desk—is a solid and permanent communication, one that can be copied and studied and read and memorized and translated and taken to the far corners of the globe, and it can be passed to the next generation.

How wise of God to give us the Holy Bible! All Scripture is given by inspiration of God (2 Timothy 3:16), and it conveys the message of eternal life.

Our Salvation Is Claimed by Faith

John's gospel is particularly important in that regard, for it has the distinct purpose of telling us that our salvation, which is centered in Christ and communicated in Scripture, is claimed by faith, and by faith alone; and that's the third part of John's purpose statement in John 20:30, 31—"And truly Jesus did many other signs in the presence of His disciples, which are not written in this book; but these are written that you may *believe* that Jesus is the Christ, the Son of God, and that *believing* you may have life in His name" (emphasis mine).

This is John's great theme. Recently, I read through the gospel of John looking for occurrences of those words *belief* and *believe* and *believing*. I couldn't believe how prominent and repetitious they were. I found exactly 101 times in which those words popped up in this gospel. I don't have space to trace all 101 occurrences, but by looking at a few of them we can see the prevalence of this theme.

- "He came to His own, and His own did not receive Him. But as many as received Him, to them He gave the right to become children of God, to those who *believe* in His name" (John 1:11, 12, emphasis mine).

- "And as Moses lifted up the serpent in the wilderness, even so must the Son of Man be lifted up, that whoever *believes* in Him should not perish but have eternal life. For God so loved the world that He gave His only begotten Son, that whoever *believes* in Him should not perish but have everlasting life. For God did not send His Son into the world to condemn the world, but that the world through Him might be saved. He who *believes* in Him is not condemned; but he who does not *believe* is condemned already, because he has not *believed* in the name of the only begotten Son of God" (John 3:14-18, emphasis mine).

● "Most assuredly, I say to you, he who hears My word and *believes* in Him who sent Me has everlasting life, and shall not come into judgment, but has passed from death into life" (John 5:24, emphasis mine).

● "Jesus answered and said to them, 'This is the work of God, that you *believe* in Him whom He sent'" (John 6:29, emphasis mine).

● "And Jesus said to them, 'I am the bread of life. He who comes to Me shall never hunger, and he who *believes* in me shall never thirst'" (John 6:35, emphasis mine).

● "And this is the will of Him who sent Me, that everyone who sees the Son and *believes* in Him may have everlasting life; and I will raise him up at the last day" (John 6:40, emphasis mine).

● "Most assuredly, I say to you, he who *believes* in Me has everlasting life" (John 6:47, emphasis mine).

- "Therefore I said to you that you will die in your sins; for if you do not *believe* that I am He, you will die in your sins" (John 8:24, emphasis mine).

- "Jesus said to her, "I am the resurrection and the life. He who *believes* in Me, though he may die, he shall live. And whoever lives and *believes* in Me shall never die. Do you *believe* this?" (John 11:25, 26, emphasis mine).

The most important question we can ever ask is this one: What must I do to be saved? The answer is: "Believe on the Lord Jesus Christ, and you will be saved" (Acts 16:31). This is the teaching of Scripture. We can never be saved from death and damnation on the basis of our own merits. It isn't going to church. It isn't trying to live a good life. It isn't works of righteousness that we do, but according to His mercy that He saves us. "For by grace you have been saved through faith, and that not of yourselves; it is the gift of God, not of works, lest anyone should boast" (Ephesians 2:8, 9). The Bible says, "If you confess with your mouth the Lord Jesus and believe in your heart that God has raised Him from the dead, you will be saved" (Romans 10:9).

What does it mean to believe in Jesus? It means to acknowledge Christ as Lord and to place your life in His hands.

Years ago, my wife and I were traveling in New Mexico with a friend. On Sunday morning we went to church and the pastor preached the sermon on this theme. At the end of his message, he told a story I had heard several times before, and I thought to myself, *That's such an old story that I can't believe he used it. Could he not find a newer and better one?* But later, the friend traveling with us said, "That was the best illustration I've ever heard of being saved by faith. I've never understood that truth as clearly as I do now."

So, with apologies to my preacher friend in New Mexico, let me tell you this well-worn story. In the 1850s there was a French daredevil with the stage name of Blondin who made several visits to Niagara Falls where he would thrill the crowds by performing feats on a high-wire stretched over the falls. One of his favorite stunts was to cross the tightrope pushing a wheelbarrow. On one occasion, he stopped at the edge of the falls to chat with the pop-eyed crowds who had gathered to watch him.

"Do you believe I can walk over the falls on this little rope?" he asked. A man in the crowd said, "Yes, certainly."

"Do you believe I can walk over the falls on this rope pushing a wheelbarrow?"

"Yes, I do believe that!" replied the man.

"Do you believe I can walk over the falls pushing a wheelbarrow with someone in it?"

"Yes," said the man. "I've seen you do it before."

"Then, kind sir," challenged the daredevil, "would you mind assisting me by getting into the wheelbarrow?"

To which the man answered: "Not on your life!"

True saving faith means getting into the wheelbarrow. It isn't just a matter of intellectual assent but of life commitment. It means that we know the content of the gospel; we believe it with our minds; and we are giving ourselves to it with our hearts and lives.

I believe the best way to do that is through prayer. When I'm with someone who wants to become a Christian, I lead them in a simple prayer expressing their faith, something like this: "Dear God, I confess my sins to You and ask for Your forgiveness. I do believe that Jesus Christ died for my sins and rose again to give me everlasting life. I here and now give Him my life and ask Him to become my Savior and Lord."

You can offer that prayer right now. Have you trusted Christ as your Savior and Lord? Are you certain? Are you in the wheelbarrow? Salvation is centered in Christ, conveyed through Scripture, and claimed by faith alone.

Simple Memory:
"These [things] are written that you may believe that Jesus is the Christ, the Son of God, and that believing you may have life in His name" (John 20:31).

2

How Can I Know for Sure?

Not long ago as I drove to a speaking engagement, I began to wonder if I was on the right road. I clutched the directions in one hand, but for some reason the route didn't feel right. I didn't have a lot of spare time, and my stomach started knotting as I told myself, "There's a seventy percent chance I'm on the right track, but a thirty percent chance I'm lost."

Just then I recognized a landmark, and all my fretting subsided. I was on the right road, and I *knew* it.

It's one thing to be traveling the road of life, but another thing to know it for sure. How terrible to journey toward heaven with anxious insecurity about our eventual destination, hoping we're on the right road but wondering if we may be lost after all.

John ended his gospel by telling us he had written it for one reason—that we might *have* eternal life. Now we find Him

16

ending his little letter of 1 John by telling us he had written it for another reason—that we might *know* we have eternal life. This five-chapter epistle tells us how we can be certain and convinced we're on the right road, that we really do have everlasting life through our Lord Jesus Christ.

"These things I have written to you who believe in the name of the Son of God," he said, "*that you may know* that you have eternal life, and that you may continue to believe in the name of the Son of God" (1 John 5:13, emphasis mine).

As I mentioned earlier, one of the things that bothers some Christians is being unable to recall the exact moment when they invited Christ into their lives. But when Jesus said, "You must be born again," He was drawing a comparison between being saved and being born. We're born a second time, this time into God's family.

So do you recall a specific incident that occurred at the time of your physical birth? Do you recall the traumatic moment when you first saw the light of day? Do you recall the face of the doctor who delivered you or the nurse who handed you to your mother? None of us remember those things, yet none of us languish in despair crying, "I'm not sure I've really been born—I can't recall a thing about it!"

We do not doubt our birth because we have three pieces of powerful evidence. First, we're breathing right now—we have air in our lungs. Second, we possess a birth certificate. Third, we bear a family likeness.

The same three indications are true for our spiritual birth. How do we know we've been born again? How can we be certain we're in God's family, heirs of His kingdom, possessors of

His life? First John stresses three tests on which we can base our assurance of salvation.

The Oxygen of the Holy Spirit

First, as Christians we have the oxygen of the Holy Spirit within us. The final sentence of 1 John 3 says: "And by this we know that He abides in us, by the Spirit whom He has given us."

In the next chapter, 1 John 4:13 adds: "By this we know that we abide in Him, and He in us, because He has given us of His Spirit."

And in the next chapter, 1 John 5:6b, "And it is the Spirit who bears witness, because the Spirit is truth."

This agrees with what we read elsewhere in Scripture. Romans 8:16, for example, says: "The Spirit Himself bears witness with our spirit that we are children of God."

Galatians 4:6 puts it like this: "And because you are sons, God has sent forth the Spirit of His Son into your hearts, crying out, 'Abba, Father!'"

In the New Testament, the apostle Paul won many people to Christ in the town of Thessalonica. Writing to them later, he said: "When we brought you the Good News, it was not just meaningless chatter to you; no, you listened with great interest. What we told you produced a powerful effect upon you, for the Holy Spirit gave you great and full assurance that what we said was true" (1 Thessalonians 1:5, TLB).

Of course, that brings up a practical question. How do you know you have the Holy Spirit living within you? Well, do you have an interest in spiritual things? Are you learning to pray? Are you getting involved in church? Do you long to please God? Is there a song in your soul? Do you feel a growing love for Jesus Christ and for others? Do you have a deepening peace? Is the Word of God meaningful to you?

All of these are the result of the inward ministry of the Holy Spirit, and these are powerful indicators that the Spirit lives within you. If none of these things are true, it's a caution flag for the soul, warning you to investigate your heart as to whether you've actually been born again.

Our Birth Certificate

Second, we know we've been saved because we have a birth certificate. When we are born literally, our names are recorded in the country of our birth and we're issued a birth certificate. Likewise, when we are born spiritually, our names are recorded in the heavenly records ("the Lamb's Book of Life," see Revelation 21:27), and the Word of God becomes our personal birth certificate.[5]

Notice how clearly this is stated in 1 John 5:11, 12—"And this is the testimony [the facts, the record, the reality, the way it is]: that God has given us eternal life, and this life is in His Son. He who has the Son has life; he who does not have the Son of God does not have life."

There's an old song that says: "Jesus loves me, this I know; / for the Bible tells me so." Our assurance of salvation is based on the unchanging Word of God.

In his book, *How to Begin the Christian Life*, George Sweeting suggests that doubting our salvation is like a prisoner who has been pardoned by the governor. A guard brings him the document, and there it is, signed and sealed. Suppose you ask the man, "Have you been pardoned?" He will say, "Yes."

"Do you feel pardoned?" we ask.

"No, I don't. It's all so sudden."

"But if you don't feel pardoned how do you know you are pardoned?"

"Oh," the man replies, "it tells me so right here."[6]

The Bible does not use vague or nonspecific language regarding our salvation. It doesn't use terms like *maybe* or *might* or *hope-to-be*. It says *will* and *shall* and *is*. If you have given your life to Jesus Christ yet still struggle with doubts about your salvation, memorize 1 John 5:11, 12—"And this is the testimony: that God has given us eternal life, and this life is in His Son. He who has the Son has life; he who does not have the Son of God does not have life."

Our Family Likeness

The third clear indication we've been truly born is our family likeness. Yesterday I saw a newborn baby, and when I looked from the baby to the mother I saw exactly the same face, just separated by age.

Likewise, when we are born again we begin to take on the characteristics and the image of Jesus Christ. We begin to grow in our resemblance and likeness to Him. This is one of the great themes of this little book of 1 John:

- 1 John 1:6 puts this in negative terms—"If we say that we have fellowship with Him, and walk in darkness, we lie and do not practice the truth." In other words, if we claim to be Christians, but there is no change in our attitudes or behavior, we're mistaken.

- 1 John 2:3—"Now by this we know that we know Him, if we keep His commandments." If our lives begin to reflect the holiness and righteousness of Jesus Christ, if there are changes in our attitudes and behavior, if there is spiritual growth taking place—then we know that we know Him.

- 1 John 2:5—"Whoever keeps His word, truly the love of God is perfected in him. By this we know that we are in Him."

- 1 John 2:29—"If you know that He is righteous, you know that everyone who practices righteousness is born of Him."

- 1 John 3:14—"We know that we have passed from death to life [that is, we know that we are really children of God, that we have really been saved], because we love the brethren."

The Bible teaches that God is love, that His love is infinite and unending, and that He loved the world so much He gave His only Son. As we grow in our Christian life, we begin to reflect God's love, learning to love even the unlovely and unlovable. That growing love is proof we've really been saved.

21

How, then, can we know we've really been saved? If we have the Holy Spirit within our spirits like oxygen, if we have the birth certificate of the Word of God, and if we're growing in our family likeness, then we can know we are saved.

If those things are not present and if there has been no change in our behavior as a result of giving our lives to Christ, then, frankly, we may not have assurance of salvation; in fact, we may not be genuinely saved.

The apostle Paul wrote these somber words in 2 Corinthians 13:5—"Examine yourselves as to whether you are in the faith. Test yourselves. Do you not know yourselves, that Jesus Christ is in you?"

There was a time in my life many years ago when I struggled with this very thing. I was raised in a Christian home and in a godly church, and while that did not make me a Christian, I can say I never knew a time when I wasn't trusting Christ. But one night—I was perhaps ten or eleven years old—we had a revival meeting at our church and the evangelist preached so hard that I questioned whether or not I had ever really been saved. After all, I could not remember a time or place when I had clearly and definitely made that decision.

That evening at bedtime, I slipped quietly into the bathroom, locked the door, and knelt down by the bathtub. I prayed something like this: "Dear Lord, I think that I have received Jesus Christ into my life by faith. If I have really done that, I thank You, Lord, for saving me. But if I have not really done that, then tonight, right here by this bathtub, I receive Him into my life as Lord and Savior."

How Can I Know for Sure?

I told no one what I had done, but I can tell you now that from that moment, I've never doubted my salvation. Perhaps you need to make a similar decision.

Simple Memory:
"This is the record: that God has given us eternal life, and this life is in His Son. He who has the Son has life; he who does not have the Son of God does not have life. These things I have written to you who believe in the name of the Son of God, that you may know that you have eternal life, and that you may continue to believe in the name of the Son of God" (1 John 5:11-13).

b = baptism.

I clearly remember the first time I officiated a baptism. The mountain church I was pastoring didn't have a baptistery, so we usually went down to the river, but in cold weather we asked a neighboring church to let us use its baptistery. A couple had joined our congregation, wanting to be baptized, and it was the winter of 1977. So we joined services with our friends down the road and during the joint evening service I baptized my first victim, er . . . person.

I thought he was a man of average size until he stood beside me in the baptistery where he suddenly seemed much larger. In fact, I was a little shocked at how tall he was, and I wasn't really sure how to go about baptizing him. As it turned out, I only had one problem—I couldn't get his nose under the water. I pushed him down a time or two, but somehow that nose just wouldn't submerge. I finally gave up, but it has distressed me all these years to know that my first baptismal candidate still has an unbaptized nose.

One of the things that most intrigues people who visit a local church like ours is this rite or ritual of baptism. It's so personal and unusual, yet so public, that those new to church naturally raise their eyebrows. Why would we take someone and plunge them into a vat of water while everyone claps and rejoices?

Baptism in the Bible

The words *baptize* and *baptism* occur exactly 100 times in the New Testament, so we know it's an important subject in the Bible. The first time we find this word in Scripture is at the beginning of the New Testament in Matthew's gospel. Before Jesus Christ began His ministry, He was preceded by John the Baptist "the Baptizer" who was His forerunner, sent by God to prepare the way. Look at Matthew 3:1-6:

> In those days John the Baptist came preaching in the wilderness of Judea, and saying, "Repent, for the kingdom of heaven is at hand!" For this is he who was spoken of by the prophet Isaiah, saying: "The voice of one crying in the wilderness: 'Prepare the way of the Lord; make His paths straight.'"
>
> Now John himself was clothed in camel's hair, with a leather belt around his waist; and his food was locusts and wild honey. Then Jerusalem, all Judea, and all the region around the Jordan went out to him and were baptized by him in the Jordan, confessing their sins.

Simple

In some ways, this was a new thing in the Bible, a new habit or ritual. Although the Old Testament contained instructions regarding various washings and cleansing ceremonies in Jewish worship, there was no Old Testament precedent, commandment, or example regarding baptism.

On the other hand, this ordinance was not actually "invented" by John. Symbolic immersion was well-known in the days of Christ. Archaeologists have found many ritual basins called *mikvahs*, dating from the first century that were used by Jewish people when preparing for worship. I recently spent several hours studying this subject at the southwestern slopes of the Jewish Temple Mount in Jerusalem. The actual remains of first century streets and shops are there, and archaeologists have excavated nearly forty *mikvahs* amid the rubble. Every Jewish person who ascended to the Temple Mount first went down into a private *mikvah* and immersed himself or herself so as to be ceremoniously cleansed before entering the temple precincts. It was a little like the Saturday night bath your mom made you take so you'd be clean for church the next morning.

Imagine the twelve disciples in Jerusalem. They never climbed the steps leading to the temple without first detouring to a private cleansing area where they formed a long line and, one by one, removed their clothes, stepped down into the *mikvah*, and submerged themselves. An adjacent set of steps led out of the pool, and after donning their clothes, they were considered ceremoniously pure for worship.

It appears, then, that while baptism is not found in the Old Testament, there were some customs pre-dating John the Baptist that were roughly similar to our New Testament practice of baptism; and when John the Baptist came baptizing, he adapted this tradition and gave it a new meaning. He said to the people of his day, in effect: "If you want to be a true Jew in your heart, if you want to be God's holy people, if you really want to belong to Him, you need to repent of your sins. And baptism in water is an outward symbol of that inward attitude of repentance, change, and cleansing."

It was just then that a most remarkable thing happened. The only person in the history of the world who needed no repentance, being sinless and pure, showed up to be baptized.

> Then Jesus came from Galilee to John at the Jordan to be baptized by him. And John tried to prevent Him, saying, "I need to be baptized by You, and You are coming to me?" But Jesus answered, "Permit it to be so now, for thus it is fitting for us to fulfill all righteousness." Then he allowed Him.
>
> When He had been baptized, Jesus came up immediately from the water; and behold, the heavens were opened to Him, and He saw the Spirit of God descending like a dove and alighting upon Him. And suddenly a voice came from heaven, saying, "This is My beloved Son, in whom I am well pleased" (Matthew 3:13-17).

After the baptism of Jesus, little more is said about baptism in the Gospels. There is a suggestion in John 4 that the disciples of Jesus baptized those coming to Him, but references to baptism are sparse until the end of our Lord's earthly ministry when He gave us a special commandment just before He returned to heaven. We call it the Great Commission.

> And Jesus came and spoke to them, saying, "All au-
> thority has been given to Me in heaven and on earth.
> Go therefore and make disciples of all the nations,
> baptizing them in the name of the Father and of the
> Son and of the Holy Spirit, teaching them to observe
> all things that I have commanded you; and lo, I am
> with you always, even to the end of the age" (Mat-
> thew 28:18-20).

After Jesus ascended into heaven, the disciples spent ten days praying and waiting before the Lord, and then on the Day of Pentecost, the Holy Spirit fell from heaven upon them as they were gathered in the Upper Room, and that is the birth of the church, which we'll look at in the next chapter. Immediately Peter started preaching the gospel, and notice what happened on that day: "Then those who gladly received his word were baptized; and that day about three thousand souls were added to them" (Acts 2:41).

In Acts 8, we have a glimpse into the way this worked in the experience of one of the early evangelists, a man named Philip, in Acts 8:26ff:

> Now an angel of the Lord spoke to Philip, saying,
> "Arise and go toward the south along the road which
> goes down from Jerusalem to Gaza." This is desert.
> So he arose and went. And behold, a man of Ethio-
> pia, a eunuch of great authority under Candace the
> queen of the Ethiopians, who had charge of all her
> treasury, and had come to Jerusalem to worship, was
> returning. And sitting in his chariot, he was reading

Isaiah the prophet. Then the Spirit said to Philip, "Go near and overtake this chariot." So Philip ran to him, and heard him reading the prophet Isaiah, and said, "Do you understand what you are reading?" And he said, "How can I, unless someone guides me?" And he asked Philip to come up and sit with him.

The place in the Scripture which he read was this [from Isaiah 53]: "He was led as a sheep to the slaughter; and as a lamb before its shearers is silent, so He opened not His mouth. In His humiliation His justice was taken away, and who will declare His generation? For His life is taken from the earth."

So the eunuch answered Philip and said, "I ask you, of whom does the prophet say this, of himself or of some other man?" Then Philip opened his mouth, and beginning at this Scripture, preached Jesus to him.

Now as they went down the road, they came to some water. And the eunuch said, "See, here is water. What hinders me from being baptized?" Then Philip said, "If you believe with all your heart, you may." And he answered and said, "I believe that Jesus Christ is the Son of God."

So he commanded the chariot to stand still. And both Philip and the eunuch went down into the water, and he baptized him. Now when they came up out of the water, the Spirit of the Lord caught Philip away, so that the eunuch saw him no more; and he went on his way rejoicing.

Simple

This tells us several things about baptism.

First, it's *biblical*. The Bible commands it and commends it; to the best of our knowledge everyone who decided to follow Christ in the New Testament was baptized as a sign and symbol of his or her decision. Second, it's *basic*; it's one of the first things that happens after a person decides to follow Christ. Third, it is *beneficial*. The new Ethiopian Christian went on his way rejoicing. There is something about baptism that is good for the soul and good for the church.

But here's the question. What exactly does it mean today? Why is baptism the great, biblical sign of conversion to Christ? Why did Jesus not select some other symbol? I can think of several ways in which we could symbolically announce our decision to follow Christ.

- On the day of our conversion, we could go out and purchase a pure white wardrobe to wear, indicating our new life in Christ.

- We could have a ceremony, similar to a wedding ceremony in which we stand in the presence of family and friends and publicly state our vows to Christ.

- We could have a ritual in which we take some object or treasure from our past life without Christ and burn it as a symbol of leaving the past behind.

- We could light a candle or recite a poem or sing a hymn or write a letter of testimony.

b = baptism

If we sat down and thought about it for a while, we could come up with lots of possible rituals or ceremonies to symbolize our new life in Christ. Why, then, did the Bible select this procedure of baptism in water?

There Is Only One Real Baptism

In answering that question, I need to make a couple of observations. First, there is only one true baptism. Let's go back to Matthew's gospel, chapter 20. In this passage, the disciples are arguing about which one of them was most important, and they even got their mothers involved. Look at verses 20ff:

> Then the mother of Zebedee's sons came to Him with her sons, kneeling down and asking something of Him. And He said to her, "What do you wish?" She said to Him, "Grant that these two sons of mine (James and John) may sit, one on Your right hand and the other on the left, in your Kingdom." But Jesus answered and said, "You do not know what you ask. Are you able to drink the cup that I am about to drink, and be baptized with the baptism that I am baptized with?"

Jesus said something similar in Luke 12:50, "I have a baptism to be baptized with, and how distressed I am till it is accomplished!"

The actual word for baptism used in the New Testament comes from the Greek term *baptizo*, which means, literally, "to plunge." Jesus was saying, "I am about to be plunged into a vat of anguish and suffering such as the world has never seen. I am about to undergo a level of pain that exceeds human endurance."

He was talking about the cross. The *only real baptism* took place on the cross of Jesus Christ and in the tomb and at the Resurrection. Baptism is synonymous with the suffering and passion of Christ.

The heart and soul of the Bible and the pivotal point of human history is the death, burial, and resurrection of Jesus. That's the gospel. We read in 1 Corinthians 15:3, 4: "For I delivered to you first of all that which I also received: that Christ died for our sins according to the Scriptures, and that He was buried, and that He rose again the third day according to the Scriptures."

Notice the three phases of our Lord's baptism into suffering. First, He died for our sins. In a newspaper article about the movie *The Passion of the Christ*, someone asked why Mel Gibson, the movie's producer, didn't have a role in his own movie. The answer was, he did. It was a cameo of sorts, for it was evidently Gibson's hand that held the nail that was pounded into the hand of Christ. It was Gibson's way of saying, "It was my sin that sent Him to the cross."

The three greatest apostolic writers in the New Testament—Paul, Peter, and John—all affirm this truth:

- Paul wrote that in Christ, God was reconciling the world to Himself (2 Corinthians 5:18). He was making peace by the blood of His cross (Colossians 1:19).

b = baptism

- Peter wrote, "For Christ also suffered once for sins, the just for the unjust, that He might bring us to God" (1 Peter 3:18). He Himself bore our sins in His own body on the tree (1 Peter 2:24).

- John wrote, "He Himself is the propitiation (the atoning sacrifice) for our sins, and not for ours only but also for the whole world" (1 John 2:2).

When Jesus spoke of His baptism into suffering, it was for the sins of all the world, your sins and my sins, that we might be forgiven and cleansed, becoming children of God and heirs of eternal life. The death, burial, and resurrection of Jesus Christ, then, is the ultimate baptism in Scripture. There is only one real baptism in this sense, for no other name exists under heaven whereby we must be saved. There is no other Savior, and no other answer to sin or death.

There Are Two Symbolic Baptisms

A symbol is a visible sign of an invisible reality. There are two symbolic baptisms in Scripture that re-create and re-enact that real baptism. The first is the water baptism of Christ at the hands of John the Baptist as we've already seen. I've been a Christian for nearly fifty years and a pastor for nearly thirty years, and it was only on a recent evening as I studied this subject in the Bible that I saw this as I had never seen it before.

It hit me as I was studying the article on baptism by Dr. Geoffrey W. Bromiley in the *Evangelical Dictionary of Theol-*

ogy. The water baptism of Christ was a pre-enactment at the very beginning of His ministry of what was going to take place at the end of His ministry. It was a prophecy. It was a type, a proto-type, of Calvary. It could even be called the last of the great Old Testament types. Jesus was "typing" Himself. It was a foreshadowing of the cross.[7]

When He stood in the water, He was standing upright in the river, just as He would later hang upright for the sins of the world. When He was lowered into the water, it was symbolic of His death and burial. When He was raised out of the water, it was a pre-enactment of His resurrection from the tomb.

Think of it! The first thing Jesus did in His earthly ministry was to provide a vivid symbol of what would take place at the climax of His earthly years. He was previewing His passion—His death, burial, and resurrection. He was telling the world in advance what He was going to do for us on the cross.

The second symbolic baptism is ours—the ordinance of baptism we observe Sunday after Sunday in our churches, and it coveys a similar meaning. When Jesus was baptized, it was in *anticipation* of what He was going to do. When we are baptized, it is in *commemoration* of what He has already done. It announces to all the world that we are identifying ourselves publicly with the death, burial, and resurrection of Christ.

Romans 6:3, 4 makes this clear: "Do you not know that as many of us as were baptized into Christ Jesus were baptized into His death? Therefore we were buried with Him through baptism into death, that just as Christ was raised from the dead by the glory of the Father, even so we also should walk in newness of life."

b = baptism

I often explain baptism by holding my ink pen in a vertical position and explaining that Jesus died in a vertical position, which is, frankly, unusual. It's fallen my lot as a minister to occasionally be present with those on their deathbeds, and everyone who has ever died in my presence has done so in a horizontal position. But Jesus was suspended upright, hanging between heaven and earth, His arms outstretched, His anguished eyes looking at the masses huddled beneath Him until finally His labored breathing ceased.

His body was then pried from the wood and He was quickly wrapped in a shroud and buried. At this point, I move my pen into a horizontal position. He was laid on a stone slab inside a first century tomb. Three days later, He was vertical again, risen, alive, resurrected in glory. I signify that by returning my pen to a vertical position.

When someone says, "I believe that Jesus Christ died, was buried, and rose again for me," and when that person receives the free gift of eternal life, how do we outwardly communicate that internal decision? We stand vertically in the water to be lowered into the watery tomb and resurrected out of it. It is a re-enactment of the death, burial, and resurrection of Christ.

There is only one real baptism, and that is the baptism of Jesus Christ on the cross when He was plunged into the depths of human anguish for our sins. There are two symbolic baptisms, both of which portray the passion of Christ. Our Lord's baptism in water *looked forward* to the cross, and our baptism in water *looks back* at the cross. When we are baptized, it epitomizes the most basic and introductory witness of our lives, and not of ours only. Everyone who came to

Christ in the New Testament, to the best of our knowledge from studying the Bible, was baptized—and went on their way rejoicing.

Have you come to Christ for forgiveness? Have you been baptized? Are you going on your way rejoicing?

Simple Memory:
"Therefore we were buried with Him through baptism into death, that just as Christ was raised from the dead by the glory of the Father, even so we also should walk in newness of life" (Romans 6:4).

4

Why Should I Get Wet?

Questions About Being Baptized

I read this newspaper story some time ago:

Natick police yesterday ruled accidental the drowning Friday of an unemployed Dorchester man who apparently lost his balance and fell into deep water while being baptized in Lake Cochituate. John E. Blue, 37, who was living at the Jesus Nazareth Holiness Church at 3 Bowdoin St., was pronounced dead at Leonard Morse Hospital in Natick shortly after the 11:30 am accident. Rev. Harold G. Branch of the church said he was baptizing Blue in waist-deep water near Rte. 9 when the two men lost their balance and fell backward. Police said the lake bottom drops off sharply immediately behind the spot where they were standing.

For obvious reasons, I seldom mention that story when baptizing someone, but I often think of it. What would it be like, I wonder, to go under the water on earth and come up from the water in heaven?

In a sense, that's what we do. When we're baptized we're signifying our death to the world and our new life in Christ. Of course, we want to keep it a symbol, not a literal event! But in considering the act of baptism, you may have some questions. Through the years I've been asked about baptism from every angle, and here are some of the questions and answers I've fielded, which might be helpful to you.

Question #1

What Am I Saying Through Baptism?

Baptism is a testimony. It sends a signal to others. It's a way of preaching a wordless sermon that communicates our new life to others.

First, we are saying, "I am identifying myself with Christ. He died and rose again, and in re-enacting His death and resurrection, I am expressing my personal commitment to follow Him." Romans 6:4 makes this clear: "We were buried with Him through baptism into death, that just as Christ was raised from the dead by the glory of the Father, even so we also should walk in newness of life."

Second, we are saying, "I have been washed from my sins." In the Old Testament, water was used in purification rites, and when John the Baptist came preaching repentance, he made a connection between repentance, and being cleansed from sin, and baptism.

Why Should I Get Wet?

There's an obvious sense, after all, in which baptism is analogous to bathing. It conveys the idea of washing away. One place in the Bible makes this crystal clear—the description of the baptism of Saul of Tarsus who became Paul the apostle. Paul recounted the experience in Acts 22:12-16:

> Then a certain Ananias, a devout man according to the law, having a good testimony with all the Jews who dwelt there, came to me; and he stood and said to me, "Brother Saul, receive your sight." And at that same hour I looked up at him. Then he said, "The God of our fathers has chosen you that you should know His will, and see the Just One, and hear the voice of His mouth. For you will be His witness to all men of what you have seen and heard. And now why are you waiting? Arise and be baptized, and wash away your sins, calling on the name of the Lord."

Notice these words: "Be baptized, and wash away your sins." At first glance that sounds like Ananias is saying that the act of baptism itself is what washes away our sins; but we know that it's the blood of Christ alone that cleanses us from sin. Revelation 1:5 says that Jesus Himself washed us from our sins with His own blood, but baptism is symbolic of that inner, spiritual washing and cleansing that takes place.

Third, we are saying, "I have been united with the body of Christ by an act of the Holy Spirit." When Jesus was baptized in the Jordan River, the Holy Spirit descended on Him and equipped Him with power for His supernatural ministry. When Jesus prepared to go to heaven, He told His disciples, "Do not leave Jerusalem, but wait for the gift my Father promised, which you have heard me speak about. For John baptized with water, but in a few days you will be baptized with the Holy Spirit" (Acts 1:4, 5, NIV).

Ten days later, God the Father sent the Holy Spirit hurtling down from heaven like a ball of fire, and all the believers were filled with the Spirit. That dynamic, common, spiritual bond marked the birth of the church.

When you and I receive Jesus Christ as our Savior, at that moment the Holy Spirit enters our lives and we become a part of that worldwide, timeless family of God known as the church. Paul put it this way in 1 Corinthians 12:12, 13 (NIV)—"The body [the church] is a unit, though it is made up of many parts; and though all its parts are many, they form one body. So it is with Christ. For we were all baptized by one Spirit into one body—whether Jews or Greeks, slave or free—and we were all given the one Spirit to drink."

Fourth, we're saying, "I've decided to live a separated life— no turning back." "Look at 1 Corinthians 10:1, 2 (NIV)—"For I do not want you to be ignorant of the fact, brothers, that our forefathers were all under the cloud and that they all passed through the sea. They were all baptized into Moses in the cloud and in the sea."

This is referring to the miraculous parting of the Red Sea that we read about in Exodus 14. As the Israelites fled from Egypt under the leadership of Moses, they came to the Red Sea, and there they were trapped like doves in a snare. The water was in front of them, and the armies of Pharaoh were behind them. But God parted the waters, and the people of Israel escaped through those towering liquid walls to the other side. When the Egyptians tried to follow, the pillars of water collapsed and the army was drowned.

Paul described this experience as a sort of baptism for the Israelites. Now, of course, the Israelites didn't get wet—it was the Egyptians who encountered the water. In what way, then, was it a baptism for the Israelites? It marked a break from the past, a separation from their old way of life in Egypt. It symbolized their freedom from slavery. It was a new beginning for them. There was no turning back. When we "go through the water," there is a sense in which it symbolizes our turning point, like the old song that says, "The cross before me, the world behind me, no turning back, no turning back."

Here's another way to look at it. Think of baptism as you would think of a wedding ring. When a couple offers their vows to one another, they are making a commitment to belong to the other exclusively in wedded union. There follows the ring portion of the service in which each partner places a ring on the fourth finger as a symbol of those vows. When someone sees that ring, it's a testimony that sends this message: "I have entered a relationship with another person and am identifying myself with my spouse. We have entered into a new family relationship, we have forsaken all others, we belong one to the other—there is no turning back."

That's the fourfold message being preached by everyone who follows the example of our Lord Jesus in baptism. In all the world, there's no more powerful symbol or sermon than that.

Question #2

Is Baptism Necessary for Salvation?

Another question that often arises is this one: Is baptism necessary for salvation? If I sincerely ask Christ to be my Lord and Savior, but I'm not baptized, am I really going to heaven? There are some Scripture verses that can be interpreted as indicating that baptism is necessary for salvation, and many Christian groups throughout church history and in our own day believe that.

Let me suggest two answers.

First, baptism is not necessary for salvation. Suppose I visit you in your home on a Tuesday night and share the gospel. We kneel down to pray, and in prayer you sincerely ask Jesus to be your Lord and Savior. The next Sunday on your way to church to be baptized, you're hit by a car and killed. Would you go to heaven or hell?

I believe you'd go to heaven. The dying thief on the cross went to be with the Lord in Paradise though it was impossible for him to be baptized in water. The Bible says, "Not by works of righteousness which we have done, but according to His mercy He saved us" (Titus 3:5). Ephesians 2:8, 9 is a classic biblical summation of how we are saved, and the word *baptism* is nowhere to be seen, "For by grace you have been saved through faith . . . not of works."

In Acts 10, the apostle Peter went to the city of Caesarea where some Gentiles (non-Jews) wanted to become Christians. This was a novel and controversial thing, for until then Christianity had been more-or-less contained within Judaism. Peter went and preached the gospel to them, and this is what he said in verses 36-48:

Why Should I Get Wet?

The word which God sent to the children of Israel, preaching peace through Jesus Christ—He is Lord of all—that word you know, which was proclaimed throughout all Judea, and began from Galilee after the baptism which John preached: how God anointed Jesus of Nazareth with the Holy Spirit and with power, who went about doing good and healing all who were oppressed by the devil, for God was with Him. And we are witnesses of all things which He did both in the land of the Jews and in Jerusalem, whom they killed by hanging on a tree. Him God raised up on the third day, and showed Him openly, not to all the people, but to witnesses chosen before by God, even to us who ate and drank with Him after He arose from the dead. And He commanded us to preach to the people, and to testify that it is He who was ordained by God to be Judge of the living and the dead. To Him all the prophets witness that, through His name, whoever believes in Him will receive remission of sins.

Then what happened?

While Peter was still speaking these words, the Holy Spirit fell upon all those who heard the word. And those of the circumcision who believed were astonished, as many as came with Peter, because the gift of the Holy Spirit had been poured out on the Gentiles also. For they heard them speak with tongues and magnify God. Then Peter answered, "Can anyone forbid water, that these should not be baptized who have received the Holy Spirit just as we have?" And he

43

commanded them to be baptized in the name of the Lord. Then they asked him to stay a few days.

Note the order of events. They heard the gospel and believed and were saved. The Holy Spirit came upon them. By the power of the Holy Spirit, they became members of the family of God. Then Peter said, in effect, "These people are Christians now. These people have Jesus in them. They have the Holy Spirit. Furthermore, the Spirit has already baptized them into His church. They are now part of the body of Christ. Who, then, can forbid them from taking the outward step symbolizing that? Who can forbid their being baptized with water?"

Larry Dyer, in his comments on this, wrote, "The baptism of the Spirit was the saving act that came first. Water baptism followed as the outward sign of the Holy Spirit's inner work in the lives of these Gentiles. This is the norm for believers. Spiritual regeneration always occurs prior to water baptism, because it is associated with the moment of faith."[8]

So baptism is not necessary for salvation. But there's another side to the coin, and that leads to the second answer I give to the question at hand. Baptism is *not necessary* for salvation, yet baptism is *not optional*. To the best of our observation and knowledge, every person in the New Testament who decided to follow Jesus Christ was baptized. It is a universal command for Christians throughout history and around the world. Acts 2:38 says, "Repent, and be baptized, every one of you." There are no examples in the Bible of unbaptized believers, except the thief on the cross. It was a universal anticipation and joy.

Why Should I Get Wet?

Question #3

Is Immersion the Only Form of Baptism?

I believe that immersion is the preferred form of baptism for three reasons. First, the English word *baptize* is the transliteration of the Greek word *baptizo*, which was most often used to mean *to plunge* or *to dip*. In one occurrence in classical literature, the word was used to describe the sinking of a ship; in another, to describe the dipping of a ladle into liquid. Second, as we've already seen, immersion vividly portrays the Lord's death, burial, and resurrection. Third, don't forget the *mikvahs*. The ancient Hebrews of Jesus' time immersed themselves as a cleansing ritual before worshiping at the temple, and the symbol of baptism was introduced against that cultural backdrop. So, yes, I believe that immersion is the preferred form of baptism.

Question #4

Can Children Be Baptized?

Yes, if they are old enough to understand salvation. In the New Testament, entire households were baptized; and that would presumably include children. In Acts 16, for example, the apostle Paul led a businesswoman named Lydia to the Lord in the city of Philippi. Soon thereafter, the warden of the local prison was saved. In both cases, they were baptized "with their household."

It would not, however, include infants because baptism is a symbol for those who have consciously received Jesus Christ as their personal Savior by grace through faith. There is not a specific case of an infant being baptized anywhere in the New Testament, and I think a child needs to be old enough to consciously receive Jesus as his or her Savior. He or she also needs to be old enough to understand something of the symbolic message of baptism. I don't want to suggest a minimum age for baptism, but it's important to work with the parents or guardians of that child to determine the appropriate time, which may be different for every child.

Question #5

What if I've Been Baptized in the Past?

Some people, when they join a new church, wonder if they should be baptized again; and some churches even request that those joining their church from another denomination be re-baptized. If your baptism followed your salvation experience and if it was meaningful to you, I don't suggest being baptized again. If you aren't sure you were really saved when you were baptized or if it wasn't meaningful to you and you'd like to be re-baptized, your pastor will be glad to cooperate with you in that. Just ask him about it.

Question #6

What if I'm Shy and Frightened to Be in Front of People?

Jesus called us to be public about our faith and unashamed of Him. Yes, sometimes it seems frightening or intimidating, and the act of baptism may even cost some people the support of their friends or families. But we have to trust God and ask Him for the courage to be a witness for Christ. The Christian life is a life of open faith, and God has not given us the spirit of fear, but of power, of love, and of a sound mind (2 Timothy 1:7).

Why Should I Get Wet?

Question #7

How Long Should I Wait After I'm Saved?

In the New Testament, people were baptized almost as soon as they were saved. The 3,000 who were converted on the Day of Pentecost were baptized immediately on that same day. Paul baptized Lydia and the jailer immediately after their conversion. Peter baptized the Christians in Caesarea upon their profession of Christ. Philip baptized the Ethiopian Eunuch within minutes of his conversion. Different churches have different policies on this, but all in all, it's best to be baptized soon after your conversion while the excitement of your decision is still fresh.

Question #8

Exactly What Happens When I Am Baptized?

Some churches have indoor baptismal pools, and others have a choice spot at a nearby lake, ocean, or river. For churches having indoor baptistries, there will be some sort of private dressing room in which you can change either into a robe or into some presentable wash-and-wear clothes. The pastor will give you some brief instructions and have prayer with you, then you'll step with him into the baptismal pool and cross your arms across your chest, bracing your one arm with the other. The minister will say something to this effect: "In obedience to the command of our Lord Jesus Christ, I baptize you in the name of the Father, and of the Son, and of the Holy Spirit." You'll bend your knees a little and assist yourself as the pastor lowers you into the water and lifts you out. You should emerge out of the water just as joyfully and exuberantly as a dead person who is coming back to life. It's wonderfully simple, but gloriously meaningful.

Question #9

I Want to Be Baptized. What Do I Do?

If you want to be baptized, or if you'd like to talk with someone about it, call your pastor or your church office and make an appointment to talk with someone about this as soon as possible.

•   •   •

My former college roommate went to work as an associate in a church following our graduation, and one day I called him to see how he was doing. "Well," he said, "we had some excitement in our church last Sunday. The pastor had entered the baptistery in advance of the candidates, and he reached up to adjust the microphone. He was nearly electrocuted and he was rushed to the hospital. He's going to be all right, but we were all . . . well, shocked."

Their shock was nothing compared to his; but in a spiritual sense, baptism should be an emerging, electrifying experience for everyone who participates. It's a once-in-a-lifetime opportunity for us to personally re-enact the death, burial, and resurrection of Jesus Christ for all to see. It's our chance to be buried with Christ in death and raised to walk in newness of life.

> **Simple Memory:**
> *"I have been crucified with Christ; it is no longer I who live, but Christ lives in me; and the life which I now live in the flesh I live by faith in the Son of God, who loved me and gave Himself for me" (Galatians 2:20).*

5

C = church.

I read of a man who dreamed of a city filled with splendid and notable buildings: great granite temples of finance and commerce where business was transacted, marble halls where university classes met, and ornate homes for the people of that city. Along the roadside was a humble structure into which men and women were coming and going.

A hundred years passed in his dream, and the man found himself in the same city, but the buildings had been torn down and rebuilt. They were even taller and more impressive. Yet, in the middle of them was the same small white structure into which people were coming and going with joy on their faces.

A thousand years passed in the man's dream, and again he saw the same city. It was a complete transformation, for the old buildings had vanished and new buildings with innovative architecture and marvelous grandeur had taken their places—all except that little frame building along the road into which men, women, and children were coming and going with joy and satisfaction on their faces.

"What is that building?" the man asked a stranger in his dream.

"That building?" said the stranger. "That represents the church, the house of God. Cities and societies rise and fall, but the church remains steadfast through the ages to assist God's people along the road of life."[9]

Virtually everyone in America knows the word *church*, but not everyone has the same idea about what a church is or what churches are supposed to do.

The most basic thing we can say about "church" is, my story notwithstanding, the church is not a building. It's a group of people who know Jesus Christ as Savior. They may meet in a building, or they may meet in a cave or under a tree; but the building itself is not the church. It's simply the meeting place for Christians.

The word *church* occurs 110 times in the New Testament, and it's a translation of the Greek word *ekklesia*, from the prefix *ek*, meaning *out*, and the Greek verb meaning *to call*. The word literally means "the called out ones," Christians being those who have been called out of sin to become members of a new family and citizens of a new kingdom.

No, the church isn't perfect; and yes, it has its share of hypocrites. Every church is made up of people from various backgrounds, possessing various levels of maturity or immaturity. In fact, every single Christian on earth is a hypocrite to some extent for our beliefs are richer than our behavior. We're pardoned, but we aren't yet perfect. We're under construction, but construction sites are seldom pretty spots.

Sometimes when I'm tempted to grow discouraged by my church, I think of something I once read: When the church first began on earth, the pastor was being executed as a criminal; the chairman of the board was out cursing and swearing that he had never even been a part of it. The treasurer was committing suicide. Most of the rest of the board members had run away. And about the only ones who showed any signs of faithfulness were a few ladies from the women's auxiliary.[10]

That's talking about Christ, Peter, Judas, and the other disciples of our Lord. Yet, just look at how God eventually used them to change the world. Don't expect the church to be perfect; just jump right in and get involved. Take the initiative. Introduce yourself. Be friendly. Find a place of service. Stop complaining about negative issues and start campaigning for positive growth. In the process, let's always remember the patterns given in the book of Acts for healthy churches.

How Did Our Church Begin?

After our Lord's death and resurrection in Jerusalem, Jesus tarried on earth forty days, during which one question was paramount on the minds of the disciples. Now what?

They thought to themselves: We know Jesus is the Messiah, the Christ, the Redeemer of Israel. We know He's the fulfillment of the Old Testament prophecies and types. We know He's the King of the Jews, the King of Israel, and the King of Kings. We know He's destined to rule on the throne of David. So what's next? What's He going to do now? How will these promises be fulfilled in Israel?

"Therefore, when they had come together, they asked Him, saying, 'Lord, will you at this time restore the kingdom to Israel?'" (Acts 1:6).

The last thing on their minds was that Jesus would suddenly leave and be gone 2000-plus years. They didn't yet comprehend that Jesus was going to return to heaven for an epoch of time, leaving them to evangelize the world while He was gone. They had no idea there would be a gap between His first and second comings; and, in fact, they didn't actually understand that there were going to be two distinct comings. The Old Testament prophets had not understood that. It was a mystery that wasn't revealed until later.

So the disciples were brimming with questions about the immediate fulfillment of the Messianic promises while Jesus was on earth during their lifetime. Having conquered death, hell, and the grave, they expected Him to conquer Israel, Rome, and Caesar. "Lord, are you at this time going to restore the kingdom to Israel?"

In His reply in Acts 1:7, Jesus did not say *Yes* or *No*. Instead He told them, "It is not for you to know times or seasons which the Father has put in His own authority."

In other words, Jesus was saying that all the great prophecies will eventually be fulfilled, though not necessarily right now. The Almighty God has His own timetable. He is first going to take My followers, group them together in a body, pour His Holy Spirit on them, create an entity called the church, and send them out to evangelize the world—that is going to happen first. Jesus put it this way in Acts 1:7ff:

c = church

> And He said to them, "It is not for you to know times
> or seasons which the Father has put in His own au-
> thority. But you shall receive power when the Holy
> Spirit has come upon you; and you shall be witness-
> es to Me in Jerusalem, and in all Judea and Samaria,
> and to the end of the earth." Now when He had spo-
> ken these things, while they watched, He was taken
> up, and a cloud received Him out of their sight.

This event, which we call the Ascension of Christ, occurred on the eastern flank of Jerusalem on the ridge of the Mount of Olives, and it totally bewildered the astounded disciples. For a long time, they gazed in stunned disbelief into the sky, trying to see the disappearing Savior. Finally two angels were sent to break the men from their reverie. "Men of Galilee," they said, "why do you stand gazing up into heaven? This same Jesus, who was taken up from you into heaven, will so come in like manner as you saw Him go into heaven" (Acts 1:11).

Coming to their senses, the disciples crossed the Kidron Valley and returned to the city where they retreated to an upper room. There were about 120 of them in all. For ten days they waited and prayed and praised God and planned for the future as best they could.

Then on the Jewish Day of Pentecost, the heavenly Father sent the Holy Spirit like a bolt of lightning to strike this group of men and women, to inflame them, and to create a new entity, which came to be called the church.

> When the Day of Pentecost had fully come, they
> were all with one accord in one place. And suddenly
> there came a sound from heaven, as of a rushing

53

mighty wind, and it filled the whole house where they were sitting. Then there appeared to them divided tongues, as of fire, and one sat upon each of them. And they were all filled with the Holy Spirit and began to speak with other tongues, as the Spirit gave them utterance.

And there were dwelling in Jerusalem Jews, devout men, from every nation under heaven. And when this sound occurred, the multitudes came together, and were confused, because everyone heard them speak in his own language. Then they were all amazed and marveled, saying to one another, "Look, are not all these who speak Galileans? And how is it that we hear, each in our own language in which we were born? Parthians and Medes and Elamites, those dwelling in Mesopotamia, Judea and Cappadocia, Pontus and Asia, Phrygia and Pamphylia, Egypt and the parts of Libya adjoining Cyrene, visitors from Rome, both Jews and proselytes, Cretans and Arabs—we hear them speaking in our own tongues the wonderful works of God" (Acts 2:1-11).

Notice the overarching point. The Father honored the promise of the Son to send the Spirit to indwell these new Christians both individually and corporately. In other words, when I became a Christian, the Holy Spirit came to live within me, and He united me with a group of other people who have the Holy Spirit living in them. Together we are the temple of the Holy Spirit.

c = church

A church, then, is a group of people committed to Jesus Christ who are bound together by the indwelling influence of the Holy Spirit.

Many people are intrigued by the matter of the various tongues or languages referred to here in Acts 2. For a few minutes at least, these 120 Christians had the ability to proclaim the gospel in the languages of the international visitors who were in Jerusalem on that day. It was a sign, a symbol, signifying that now the age of the church had begun. It was the age of grace, the epoch of the gospel, the era in which the Good News of Jesus Christ would be taken—not just to the Jewish nation—but to every tribe and tongue and territory on the face of the earth. To this day, the great task of the church is to proclaim the gospel to every language group on earth.

The church was born on the Day of Pentecost in Acts 2, and its mission is to spread the news about Jesus until that moment when He will return to restore the kingdom to Israel and to take His place on David's throne.

What Is Our Church Like?

The second chapter of Acts goes on to tell us about the growth of the church. The events in this chapter occurred on a Jewish holy day—the Day of Pentecost—and thousands of people were there. The old walled city of Jerusalem was not a particularly large place (it still isn't), so the people were jam-packed into close quarters. When this commotion and phenomenon occurred, people came running, thousands of them, to see what was happening; and the apostle Peter took the occasion to preach the gospel. His sermon makes up the middle of Acts 2, and look at the way he ended his message in verse

55

36: "'Therefore let all the house of Israel know assuredly that God has made this Jesus, whom you crucified, both Lord and Christ.' Now when they heard this, they were cut to the heart, and said to Peter and the rest of the apostles, 'Men and brethren, what shall we do?'"

Peter's reply summarized for all of time the great message of the church. He said:

> Repent, and let every one of you be baptized in the name of Jesus Christ for the remission of sins; and you shall receive the gift of the Holy Spirit. For the promise is to you and to your children, and to all who are afar off, as many as the Lord our God will call.
>
> And with many other words he testified and exhorted them, saying, "Be saved from this perverse generation." Then those who gladly received his word were baptized; and that day about three thousand souls were added to them. And they continued steadfastly in the apostles' doctrine and fellowship, in the breaking of bread, and in prayers. Then fear came upon every soul, and many wonders and signs were done through the apostles. Now all who believed were together, and had all things in common, and sold their possessions and goods, and divided them among all, as anyone had need.
>
> So continuing daily with one accord in the temple, and breaking bread from house to house, they ate their food with gladness and simplicity of heart, praising God and having favor with all the people. And the Lord added to the church daily those who were being saved (Acts 2:40-47).

c = church

This passage presents two spheres of church life. Let's call the first "Big Church." Acts 2:46 says, "So continuing daily with one accord in the temple. . . ." The temple was the largest building in Jerusalem and it had lots of courtyards, halls, rooms, and chambers. It had been renovated and enlarged by King Herod, and it was one of the most magnificent buildings on earth. On the southern flank was a magnificent portico, capable of accommodating large numbers of people for public meetings. On a regular basis, hundreds and thousands would gather there for worship.

That's what happens every weekend at my church and yours. Scores, hundreds, or thousands gather to worship God, to sing His praises, to pray together, to hear His Word, and to honor, glorify, and adore our Lord Jesus Christ.

This means so very much to me. Some of my earliest childhood memories are sitting on the hard pews of our church in Elizabethton, Tennessee. I remember seeing my dad and mom up in the choir. I recall our pastor, Rev. Winford R. Floyd, preach the Bible to us. He would often weep during his sermons, and he preached with intelligence, passion, and conviction. I don't remember many of his individual sermons, but the cumulative effect of hearing him preach Sunday after Sunday for all the years of my childhood was profound.

I remember how we would often close the service with baptisms. After the sermon and the invitation, Pastor Floyd would excuse himself, call for those who were to be baptized to follow him, and then they all retired to the dressing rooms while the rest of us sang "Shall We Gather at the River." In a few minutes, they would come into the baptismal pool to give public demonstration of their faith in Christ.

Simple

I recall hearing people stand to share their testimonies. There was an older woman named Pearl McGee who sat right behind us most Sundays. She wasn't a particularly outgoing woman, but occasionally she would stand to share a word of testimony; and she always spoke with so much passion she almost seemed angry. She was so vehement about what Christ had done for her that my father tried to avoid sitting directly in front of her. He sometimes complained that in her excitement she would pound his shoulders while testifying.

Now the years have passed, and as time goes by the songs change a little and the form changes a little and the faces and names change. But in general, when we gather on Sunday, we're doing exactly what Christians have done for hundreds of years. We sing and pray and preach and baptize and observe the Lord's Supper and give thanks and say with the psalmist, "I was glad when they said to me, 'Let us go into the house of the LORD'" (Psalm 122:1).

That's "Big Church." But there's a second sphere of church life in Acts 2, which we can call "Small Church." Verse 46 says, "So continuing daily with one accord in the temple, and breaking bread from house to house, they ate their food with gladness and simplicity of heart."

They would not only gather en masse in the temple, they would break into smaller groups that met in each other's homes. That's where the more personal friendships developed. That's where they could bear one another's burdens and meet one another's needs. Today we often do this in Sunday School classes or Bible study groups.

A healthy "Big Church" opens the front door to guests, for most visitors and prospects make their first entrance to our church during our Sunday services. A healthy "Small Church" closes the back door, because as people are loved and cared for they are less likely to drop out. It's in these small, loving groups that prayer and pastoral care occur, allowing us to meet each other's needs through the grace of Christ Jesus.

A couple of years ago, my wife and I vacationed in California and visited the national parks that are filled with redwood trees. They are so old that some were standing during the days of Christ, and they're considered the largest things on earth, towering hundreds of feet above the forest floor. You might think that trees that large would have a root system reaching hundreds of feet into the earth, but the redwoods actually have very shallow systems of roots. How can such tall trees remain upright when their root systems are relatively shallow? According to the park guide, they all intertwine. They are locked to each other. When the storms come or the winds blow, the redwoods stand. Their roots are interlocked, and they don't stand alone; all the trees support and protect each other. That's a picture of the relationships in "Small Church."

Both in "Big Church" and "Small Church," it's important to be faithful. Woody Allen once said, "Eighty percent of life is just showing up." That's true for church. The North Carolina evangelist Vance Havner once bemoaned, "There is something wrong with our Christianity when we have to beg most of our crowd to come to church to hear about it."[11]

How would you like it if your watch ticked one time and missed the next? Your heart beat one time and missed the next? Your child missed every other day at school? The engine of your car only hit on half its cylinders?

Irregularity in any area of life causes problems, doesn't it? Acts 2:42 says this about the early Christians: "They continued steadfastly in the apostles' doctrine and fellowship, in breaking of bread and in prayer." The book of Hebrews adds, "Let us consider one another in order to stir up love and good works, not forsaking the assembling of ourselves together, as is the manner of some, but exhorting one another, and so much the more as you see the Day approaching" (Hebrews 10:24, 25).

What's the Purpose of Our Church?

Why do all this? What's the purpose of the church? When a lawyer asked Jesus what our greatest obligations were in life, He simply said, in effect, "It's simple. Love God and love each other." We call this the Great Commandment. It's found in Matthew 22:35ff:

> One of them, a lawyer, asked Him a question, testing Him, and saying, "Teacher, which is the great commandment in the law?" Jesus said to him, "You shall love the LORD your God with all your heart, with all your soul, and with all your mind. This is the first and great commandment. And the second is like it: You shall love your neighbor as yourself. On these two commandments hang all the Law and the Prophets."

In other words, our calling is to love God and love others. See how precisely that fits with the two-fold structure of the church. What's the main purpose of "Big Church"? Loving God. When we gather for worship, we're emphasizing the vertical relationship with Him. We really don't get to know one another very well in the larger gatherings. Our seats don't face each other. We don't spend a lot of time in conversation. We're facing forward, looking upward, addressing God in song and prayer, listening as He speaks to us in His Word.

In "Small Church," on the other hand, we're more horizontal, all about building relationships with others, establishing meaningful friendships, loving each other.

Are you a part of both spheres of church life?

I read about a woman who was teaching Vacation Bible School, and her class was interrupted by a new student who entered the room. He had an arm missing, and since the class was nearly over, the teacher had no opportunity to learn the background of the little fellow; nor did she have an opportunity to talk to the other children. Being a sensitive teacher, she would have cautioned the others about saying anything to embarrass the boy.

As the class time came to a close, she asked the children to join her in their usual closing ceremony. "Let's make our churches," she said. And putting her hands together she said, "Here's the church and here's the steeple, open the doors and here's the people." Suddenly the awful truth came to her—she had done the very thing she was afraid the children would do. As she stood there speechless, the girl sitting next to the fellow reached over with her left hand and placed it up to his right hand and said, "Here, Thomas. Let's make the church together."[12]

The Lord Jesus Christ died and rose again to create a group of people, redeemed by His blood, who love God and who love each other—and then He sent them out to win the world and to build the church together. Let every one of us be a part of it!

> **Simple Memory:**
> *"Not forsaking the assembling of ourselves together, as is the manner of some, but exhorting one another, and so much the more as you see the Day approaching" (Hebrews 10:25).*

d = devotions.

I read about a little boy who said to his parents one morning, "I'm not going to get out of bed until I see Jesus." This naturally perplexed them until the little fellow pointed to a picture on the wall, which was obscured by the early morning shadows. It was a picture of Christ. He didn't want to get out of bed until the sunlight from his window fell across the face of Christ. The boy's dad later thought to himself, "None of us should start the day until we've seen Christ."

Nothing is more important to the Christian than the practice of having a daily appointment with the Lord, a regular period of daily Bible study and prayer. Some people call this daily devotions. Others, the morning watch. Still others refer to their quiet time. It's the missing ingredient in many a Christian life.

A Personal Testimony

I'm grateful to the Lord for bringing several influences into my life that helped me establish this practice when I was younger. The first influence, though I wasn't fully conscious of it at the time, was my father. As I grew up, I'd often see him reading his Bible at night; and when I was barely old enough to read, he bought me a little Bible, which I kept beside my bed, and in this way I learned as a child to read the Scriptures daily.

That didn't mean, however, that I was actively having a meaningful quiet time, and as I grew older I got away from close daily fellowship with the Lord and grew confused in life, as young people often do. In 1971, I enrolled at Columbia Bible College in South Carolina, transferring there as a sophomore. On my second night in the dorms, I surrendered my life to the Lord, and during the following weeks I began to learn the importance of quiet time.

In fact, at that time in the early 1970s, student life was regimented, and the daily quiet time was a required part of our schedule. We were awakened every morning at 6:15 by a bell loud enough to call the fire department. We had a half-hour to shower, shave (or put on make-up, depending on which side of campus you lived), and dress, then another bell would ring, signaling our quiet time. We had half an hour every morning, from 6:45 to 7:15, then a third bell would clang, sending us to breakfast.

At first I wasn't too excited about the schedule. I liked to stay up late, and sometimes I'd slump over my desk during my quiet time in a dead sleep. Then one day a man came to preach in our chapel services, and I'd never heard anyone like him. He stood in the pulpit like a machine gun, his rapid fire, crystal-clear British accent delivering brilliant expositions of interesting passages of Scripture. One day after chapel I approached him—his name was Stephen Olford—and I asked him if he had any advice for a young man contemplating going into the ministry.

"Yes," said Dr. Olford, with the same dramatic delivery I'd heard in the pulpit. "Yes," he said, "I do. Never, never, never miss your quiet time."

That's all he said. But that was enough. I began to realize that there must be something pretty important about this half-hour between the bells.

It was shortly after that when another influence came into my life, an older woman who was well-known for her wit and wisdom Mrs. Ruth Bell Graham. One day she said, "Robert, do you have the notebook habit?" I didn't know what the notebook habit was, so I said no, I didn't think I did. She told me about her little loose-leaf notebook made of leather. She said she kept wearing it out, but she had a leather crafter who kept repairing it for her.

In her little notebook, she would record the insights God gave her each day as she studied her Bible. That very day I drove into town, found a stationary shop, and bought a notebook, and began using it as a sort of journal for my quiet time, a practice that I've followed ever since.

Then I came upon another set of influences, for I developed an interest in Christian biography. Over and over as I read about the lives and ministries of great Christian men and women, I discovered they had one thing in common. They maintained a quiet time habit.

- Missionary and author **Isobel Kuhn**, in her book *In the Arena*, wrote about a time when she was a student at Moody Bible Institute and found herself so busy that she was in danger of quenching her devotional life. Other students were facing similar problems. So they met together and Isobel suggested they sign a covenant—not a vow, but a statement of intention: "I suggested our making a covenant with the Lord to spend an hour a day (for about a year) in the Lord's presence, in prayer or reading the Word. The purpose was to form the habit of putting God in the centre of our day and fitting the work of life around Him, rather than letting the day's business occupy the central place and trying to fix a quiet time with the Lord somewhere shoved into the odd corner or leisure moment." Only about nine people signed the covenant to begin with, but the news spread and others began to join. For Isobel, the major problem was finding a quiet place. She wrote, "The only place I could find where I would disturb no one was the cleaning closet! So each morning I stole down the hall, entered the closet, turned the scrubbing pail upside down, sat on it, and with mops and dust rags hanging around my head, I spent a precious half-hour with the Master. The other half-hour had to be found at the end of the day."[13]

- Another missionary to China, **Bertha Smith**, wrote an absolutely fascinating story of her life. It was bitterly cold in her part of China. During the day she wore thirty pounds of clothing, and at night she slept under heavy bedding and with a hot water bottle. But her challenge came in the early

d = devotions

morning hour when she wanted to rise before others so she could have her quiet time before the scores of interruptions that each day brought. She would struggle in the darkness to put on her layers of clothing, then break the ice to wash her face in the cold water. Slipping out to a particular haystack, she would rake aside the frosted part of the hay, kneel down, and spend time with the Lord before the sun came up.[14]

- The great Puritan, **Thomas Watson**, practiced a similar habit. He wrote: "The best time to converse with God is before worldly occasions stand knocking at the door to be let in: The morning is, as it were, the cream of the day, let the cream be taken off, and let God have it. Wind up thy heart towards heaven at the beginning of the day, and it will go the better all the day after."[15]

- Here is what a biographer said of **William Carey**, the "Father of Modern Missions," who served many years in the land of India: "In the walled garden of the mission house at Serampore, he built an arbor which he called his 'bower.' There at sunrise, before tea, and at the time of full moon when there was the least danger from snakes, he meditated and prayed, and the Book which he ceaselessly translated for others was his own source of strength and refreshment."[16]

- A well-known British statesman, the late **Earl Cairns**, Lord Chancellor of England, was an extremely busy man, but no matter what time he reached home in the evening, he always arose at the same hour to have his quiet time the next morning. His wife said, "We would sometimes get home from Parliament at two o'clock in the morning, but Lord Cairns would always arise at the same hour to pray and study the Bible."[17] He later attributed his success in life to this practice.

- This is what a biographer wrote about evangelist **D. L. Moody**: "He was an early riser. He generally rose about daybreak in summer, devoting the early hours to Bible study and communion with God. He used to say that one who followed this plan could not get more than twenty-four hours away from God."[18]

- Of **Dr. Campbell Morgan**, I read: "Here was a man who coveted for himself a constant withdrawal from the pressing demands of his busy life, and kept inviolate the sanctity of the early morning vigil of prayer and meditation. Here he breathed the atmosphere of heaven, and daily recharged his spirit with the power that in turn poured out in extravagant measure in the preaching and proclamation of the Word."[19]

- In the biography of missionary physician, **L. Nelson Bell**, John Pollock writes: "Most important of all was Nelson Bell's discipline of devotional life. Early every morning he had a cup of coffee and went to his desk for about an hour of Bible study and prayer. He set himself to master the content and meaning of the Bible, devising such study schemes as looking up every Old Testament reference which occurs in the New Testament and typing it out. Then he turned to prayer, for friends, colleagues, and patients, praying especially for every patient listed for operation that day."[20]

Spurred by these influences, I've maintained the quiet time habit since 1971. I can't say that I've never missed a day, because I have. Occasionally I still do. But by and large, it has long been a well-established and precious pattern in my life, and I consider this the most important habit I've ever developed.

A Biblical Mandate

Now what does the Bible say on this subject? A personal testimony is worthless unless it's validated by the authority of Scripture. Let's begin with the statesman/prophet Daniel, famous for his adventure in the lions' den. At the time of this incident, Daniel was old, and everyone knew of his lifelong faithfulness to a daily schedule of devotions. His political enemies schemed against him by persuading the king to issue a one-month prohibition against praying.

> "Now when Daniel knew that the writing [the prohibition] was signed, he went home. And in his upper room, with his windows open toward Jerusalem, he knelt down on his knees three times that day, and prayed and gave thanks before His God, as was his custom since early days" (Daniel 6:10).

Notice those seven words: "As was his custom since early days." This was a lifelong habit. I suppose Daniel rose early each morning for his quiet time, then went to his office and worked through the morning before coming home at lunch where he also found a few minutes for prayer. Perhaps in that culture they prolonged the luncheon hour as a siesta because of the oppressive heat in the middle of the day, and this gave Daniel some time to spend with the Lord. Then at the close of day, his work behind him, he spent time with the Lord before going to bed. That was his lifelong habit.

Now look at the example of one greater than Daniel in Mark 1:35, "Now in the morning, having risen a long while before daylight, [Jesus] went out and departed to a solitary place; and there He prayed."

Notice how Jesus put it in Matthew 6:6, "But you, when you pray, go into your room, and when you have shut your door, pray to your Father who is in the secret place; and your Father who sees in secret will reward you openly."

The old versions say, "Go into your closet." My wife and I once visited the London home of John Wesley, the famous evangelist and the founder of the Methodist movement. On the second floor was Wesley's bedroom, and attached to the bedroom was a little room about the size of a closet with nothing in it except a small table and chair and a little window. This was Wesley's prayer closet, and it was called the powerhouse of Methodism.

The actual Greek word Matthew used for "closet" was *tameion*. It occurs four times in the New Testament, and it means a storage room, a pantry, a spare stable in the barn, or a root cellar. In those days, large families tended to live together in rather small houses. There was very little privacy. The only room not inhabited would be the storage room. Jesus was advising us to find a quiet, private place and use it as a place to meet secretly with the God of this universe. That's what the quiet time is.

I have two words of warning, however. First, it's important to realize that a daily quiet time does not represent the totality of our fellowship with God. It doesn't mean that we can meet God in the morning and then leave Him there in the closet while we go into the day. The Bible tells us to pray without ceasing. In other words, communion and fellowship with God is the constant privilege of the Christian.

Earlier I mentioned something Dr. Stephen Olford had said to me when I was a college student. Decades later, just before he went home to be with the Lord, I met him again; and once again, I asked him about his daily quiet time. We had more time to talk, and he went into detail.

"I have a very, very simple procedure," he said. "I read from Genesis to Revelation. When I reach Revelation I go back to Genesis. Even though I have read it over the years—over and over and over again—never a morning with God that He does not reveal something new to me. I read the passage three times: First time generally, second time expositionally, third time personally. I let the Lord speak to me, showing me in His Word a promise to keep, a prayer to echo, a command to obey, a sin to confess, etc. I personalize it entirely and write in that form. And then I like to take what I have written and loosely turn that into prayer so that my prayers are not mechanical. It is not a Chinese wheel I can just put on. It is a prayer that comes right out of my quiet time before I go into thanksgiving, intercessions, etc."

Then I asked him if he kept a prayer list. He replied, "Yes! My prayer list is a very interesting one. Monday—Missions. Tuesdays—Thanksgiving. Wednesday—Workers, staff, etc. Thursday—Tasks. Friday—Family. Saturday—Saints (so much of Paul's praying was for the saints). And Sunday—Sinners. On the list of sinners for this present period of my life, one of them is a famous golfing figure that I'm praying for earnestly, because I believe if he were converted it would turn the youth world upside down. Anyway, I do have a prayer list, and under those headings. Now, it isn't the length of time I spend in my quiet time, though I usually take an hour, but there is a carry-over of the activity of prayer, the attitude of prayer, that marks the rest of the day. I never pick up a telephone without a prayer. I never dictate a letter to my secretary without a prayer. I never let anybody into my study or out of my study without a prayer, and as my beloved workers know, any time we get together we say, 'Let's pray.' And so, prayer is literally praying without ceasing. At the drop of a hat . . . and so I feel I live in that of perpetual prayer."

All of which is to say, the quiet time is not the totality of our fellowship or communion with Christ. Instead, it sets the stage for it all day long.

Here's my second caution. It's important to realize that a daily quiet time is not simply a routine or a ritual. It's a relationship. We meet Christ at the *cross*, and we call that *conversion*. We meet with Him in the *closet*, and we call that *conversa-*

tion. At the cross is where we come to *know Christ*, and in the closet is where we come to *know Him better*.

Exodus 33:11 says that Moses met with the Lord face to face, as a man speaks with his friend. The quiet time is essentially a conversation, a time of fellowship, a daily meeting or appointment with the Lord. It isn't a complicated thing, and the simpler we can keep it the better. It isn't even always necessary to have a Bible. Sometimes it's nice just to go for a walk and spend some time meditating on some verse of memorized Scripture, and then talking to the Lord about it and praying over the things that concern you.

Usually, however, it's very helpful to have a Bible. And remember that you aren't reading your Bible to get through a certain amount of Scripture or to prepare a sermon or to develop a Sunday School or Bible study lesson. You're going to the Bible in order to find nourishment for your soul. Psalm 37:3, 4 puts it very well when it says, "Feed on His faithfulness. Delight yourself also in the LORD." That's a good definition of the quiet time.

How Do I Do It?

Have a procedure for your quiet time. I follow a two-step plan—Scripture and prayer. First, I open God's Word and, after a brief prayer asking for His blessing, I start reading where I left off the day before. I don't try to read a certain number of verses or chapters; I just read until I find a verse that speaks to me. Right now I'm reading through the gospel of John. It may take me a couple of weeks or a couple of months, but I'm in no hurry. I just begin reading today where I left off yesterday, and

I look for that verse to underline or to jot in my notebook as my verse for the day. Then I begin praying at the point of that verse, and move into a time of prayer. For example, my verse this morning was John 1:43, "Follow Me." I began my prayer time saying something like, "Lord, help me follow You more closely," and then I prayed for my loved ones that they would follow the Lord, and from there I went into a time of prayer using my various praise and prayer lists. So that's the essence of it—a time of Bible reading and meditation followed by a time of prayer. It's a conversation. The Lord speaks to me through His Word, then I speak to Him in prayer. And it's through this sort of daily conversation that we get to know Him better.

Use a pen. As I mentioned above, I keep a little notebook. It's divided into two parts. The first part is my journal. Every morning I come to my desk with a cup of coffee and my Bible, and I open my journal and put down the date. Then I might write something about my day or how I'm feeling. I'll often summarize what happened the day before or what I'm anticipating in the day just beginning. Then I just put down the Scripture reference that I'm reading, and as I read through the passage I make notes.

Just this week, for example, in my daily Bible reading, I came to the paragraph in the first chapter of John's gospel in which he introduced Jesus Christ to the crowds. Perhaps I was just tired, but for some reason I just couldn't seem to connect to that passage. I read the same paragraph three times but not a single word registered on my brain. My mind was sluggish. I said to myself, "I've got to do better than this. There must be something here worth reading and remembering." So I picked up my pen and started to make a little list in my notebook. I listed five things John the Baptist said about Jesus Christ. I was amazed at how rich and interesting the passage became; and one day I may preach a five point sermon about Christ, based on the five things John the Baptist said in John 1:29-34.

The last half of my notebook is for my prayer lists. I have a daily list, for there are some things I want to pray about every day. Then I have a list for each day of the week. For example, if I want to pray for a particular missionary family on a weekly basis, I just take their prayer card, punch holes in it, and insert it under the Monday tab, or the Tuesday, or whatever.

I find a little notebook to be an incredible aid; but not everyone wants to keep a notebook, so here's an alternative. Try using the margin of your Bible as a kind of ad hoc journal. Suppose, for example, you are reading through the gospel of John. Beside John 1:1, put today's date. Then start there and read through the passage, marking anything that is of interest until you find just the verse that speaks to your soul for that day. Let's say that it is verse 16, "From the fullness of His grace we have all received one blessing after another" (NIV). Circle that verse and end your reading there. The next day, put the new date beside John 1:17 and read on until you find that day's verse, then circle it. And so forth.

For a prayer list, you can use the flyleaf of your Bible or a slip of paper in the back cover. Or you can just use a mental list. I'm not sure our Lord took a paper list with Him when He rose early on that morning in Capernaum and retreated to the nearby mountains. Perhaps it would work better for you just to say, "Lord, guide me today to those things You want me to pray about."

Simple

Again, simplicity is the rule. The Word of God and prayer. Going into the closet and meeting with the Father in secret. A notebook helps me, but don't feel like you have to do it the way I do. Find the method that works best for you.

Find a regular place and time. It seems that Jesus had two primary places He used as His "closet." When in the north of Israel, He'd retreat into the mountains to be alone. We saw that in Mark 1, and we also see it later when He sent His disciples by boat to the other side of the lake while He Himself went up into the mountains to pray. But where would He go when He was in Jerusalem? It was much more difficult to be alone there. John 18:1 says He went out of the city, across the Kidron Valley, and into an olive orchard that was apparently owned by a friend who gave Him access to it. I suppose the friend said, "Lord, here's the key to the gate. Feel free to relax there whenever you'd like." The place was called Gethsemane and Judas led the soldiers there to arrest Jesus. He knew Christ often went there late at night or perhaps early in the morning for His quiet time.

For you it might be the kitchen table, the front seat of your car, or your bedside at night. And that brings up another question. Does it have to be in the morning? No. If the evening is better for you, or the midnight hour, or the noon hour during lunch break, that's fine. We each need to find the routine that works for us. My suggestion is just that you have a regular time or place in order to make it habitual and regular and a part of the normal routine of your day.

Whenever I speak on this subject, another question comes up: What about those times in life when our schedules are out of control? Sometimes, despite our best efforts, we go through periods in which we have a difficult time maintaining a habit such as I've described. This is especially true of mothers of preschoolers.

In my reading, I was intrigued with the testimony of Rosalind Goforth, who was a mother and a busy missionary in China. She was very eager to maintain her quiet time habit, but she was greatly frustrated by the fact that no matter how early she got up and how quiet she tried to be, one or more of her children woke up, and the daily circus just started that much earlier. So she finally just kept a small Bible or New Testament with her all the time, and she learned to take those odd moments all through the day to memorize Scripture. That way, she had it available for meditation all day long, and she just turned each day into one long 24-hour quiet time.

I've read several magazine articles by mothers who have done that very thing. One mother with five children, ages ten months to ten years, struggled with having a routine for her quiet time until she finally went out and bought a handful of small Bibles that she kept open at various places in the house. One was by the ironing board, one was by the bathroom vanity, one was by the kitchen sink. All day long, she would catch a snitch of Scripture here and there. When she bathed the baby, she would pray for that child. When she folded clothes, she prayed for the one to whom they belonged. She kept the radio on a Christian station so that day was filled with Christian music and Bible teaching. She just turned each day into an extended quiet time.

My wife, Katrina, however, had a different idea about it. She was a stay-at-home mother with three small children, but she sat them down one day and had a talk with them. She said something to this effect, "Now, girls, I want to be a good mother who is kind and patient, but to be that way I need to spend time with the Lord each day. Every afternoon, I'm going to have my quiet time; and that's going to be your 'alone time' in your rooms. You can sleep or nap or read or play quietly by yourselves, but you're not to come and interrupt me—and if you do I'll break your necks."

I'm really not sure she said that last part, but whatever she said worked, and she was able to maintain her quiet time even during that busy phase of her life.

There's more than one way to skin a cat, and there's more than one way to have your quiet time; but all things being equal, I still think a few minutes early in the morning with a Bible, notebook, and a cup of strong, hot coffee is the best way to start the day.

Finally, *exercise perseverance.* Paderewski, one of the world's greatest pianists, said: "When I miss a day of practice, I can always tell it. If I miss two days, the critics will pick it up. If I miss three days, the audience will notice it."[21] The same is true of the quiet time.

At first, it may seem stiff and awkward; you might even wonder if you're getting much out of it. Don't give up. On some days my quiet time is more meaningful than others, but it's worthwhile every day, and if I miss a day of meeting with the Lord in prayer and Bible reading, it seems as if my entire day is off-kilter.

d = devotions

I read about an exploring party in Africa that was pushing with great intensity through the jungle and the bush. After making remarkable progress, the explorer grew frustrated when his national guides just sat down and refused to go further. He asked, "Are you tired?" Not particularly. "Are you sick?" No. "Well, why have you stopped?" Their answer was, "We must pause now to let our souls catch up with our bodies."

Why not begin the practice of daily devotions tomorrow? Better yet, why not start today!

Simple Memory:
"I rise before the dawning of the morning, And cry for help; I hope in your word. My eyes are awake through the night watches, That I may meditate on Your word" (Psalm 119:147, 148).

7

e=evangelism.

A couple of years ago while visiting a particular city, Katrina and I took a taxi, and we soon learned our driver was a Muslim gentleman from Africa. As we chatted with him, I sought to bring up the subject of Christianity and he commented there was little difference between Christianity and Islam. "Really there are only two differences," he said. "Muslims don't believe that God had a son, and Muslims don't eat pork."

Being a little surprised at his naiveté, I suggested there might be some other differences. "Like what?" he asked.

"Well, for one thing," I said, pausing to choose my words, "Mohammad is dead, and Jesus Christ is alive. He rose from the grave on the third day."

My taxi driver nodded thoughtfully and admitted that was a significant difference. And I felt the Lord had given me an opportunity to gently plant a seed of truth in the man's mind.

e = evangelism

Christians are like Johnny Appleseed. We go through each day looking for quiet ways to sow the seed of the gospel; and that is the meaning of evangelism. The very word *evangelism* is wonderful. The prefix, *ev*, means *good*. And the stem word is *angel*. We think of an angel as a supernatural being, but the original meaning was simply "messenger."

So the word *ev-angel-ism* is literally *good-message-ism*, and the word *evangelist* refers to anyone who shares the Good News with another. Mark 1:16-18 says:

> And as [Jesus] walked by the Sea of Galilee, He saw Simon and Andrew his brother casting a net into the sea; for they were fishermen. Then Jesus said to them, "Follow Me, and I will make you become fishers of men." They immediately left their nets and followed Him.

Several things impress me about this. First, there are not two commands here, but *only one*—one command and a promise. Jesus didn't say, "Follow me and fish for men." He said, "Follow Me, and I will make you become fishers of men." The act of following is something I can do. I can get behind someone else and walk in his footsteps. I can learn to follow Christ. But as far as being a fisher of men on my own, I can't do that. That intimidates me. That seems beyond my comfort zone and skill level, and I'm very aware that I can never, by my own personality or persuasiveness, change another person's heart.

Jesus didn't command me to fish for men, only to follow Him. But as I do so, He has promised *to make me to become*

His fisherman. I like the way Lorne Sanny put it when he said that fishing for men and women is our responsibility. It's our *response-ability*, our *response* to His *ability*. The response comes from us and the ability comes from Him.[22]

Think of how it worked out for those first disciples. When Jesus met them on the shores of Galilee, they were a long way from being evangelists. They were simply unlettered, fledgling men who were slowly growing in their awareness of the Lord's identity. We read of their mistakes and mis-steps throughout the gospel accounts. But by the time we get to the book of Acts, these same men are turning the world upside down.

Acts 4 describes how the apostles bravely preached the gospel before the hostile Jewish ruling counsel; and Peter proclaimed, "Nor is there salvation in any other, for there is no other name under heaven given among men by which we must be saved" (Acts 4:12). The next verse, Acts 4:13, gives the response of the audience: "Now when they saw the boldness of Peter and John, and perceived that they were uneducated and untrained men, they marveled. And they realized that they had been with Jesus."

They had followed Jesus as best they could; and Jesus had kept His promise to make them fishers of men. That's the pattern for Christians. First we're disciples (learners), then we become apostles (those who are sent). First we're followers, and then He makes us fishers. As we grow in Christ, we should become increasingly influential in leading others to Him.

There's a second observation to make about this, however. We must be aware that we're not the only ones interested in catching fish. The New Testament was originally written in the

Greek language. There is a word that only occurs twice in the Greek New Testament, the word *zogreo* (zo-gre'-o). It means "to catch, like in a net."

We first encounter the word *zogreo* in Luke 5. Here Jesus had been teaching the multitudes. The crowds were so great that Jesus got into a boat, pushed out from the shore, and taught the multitudes from the water. Then, His teaching finished for the moment, Jesus told Peter to launch further into the lake and to let down his nets. Suddenly so many fish swam into the nets that the boats were in danger of sinking.

> When Simon Peter saw it, he fell down at Jesus' knees, saying, "Depart from me; for I am a sinful man, O Lord!" For he and all who were with him were astonished at the catch of fish which they had taken; and so also were James and John, the sons of Zebedee, who were partners with Simon. And Jesus said to Simon, "Do not be afraid. From now on you will catch [*zogreo*] men" (verses 8-10).

This was a rephrasing of our Lord's promise to make Peter and the other disciples into fishers of men. You will catch (*zogreo*) men in the nets of the gospel.

This unusual word occurs one other time in the Bible, in 2 Timothy 2:24-26 where the apostle Paul is instructing Timothy on going about his ministry:

> And a servant of the Lord must not quarrel but be gentle to all, able to teach, patient, in humility correcting those who are in opposition, if God perhaps will grant them repentance, so that they may know

the truth, and that they may come to their senses
and escape the snare of the devil, having been taken
captive [*zogreo*] by him to do his will.

This word, which means to catch in a trap or in a net, occurs only twice in the New Testament. The Holy Spirit put it there to show us we're to be diligently fishing for men, for another fisherman—a diabolical personage of evil—is also trolling for men, women, boys, and girls, and he wants to catch them in his snares.

It's urgent, then, that we become fishers doing the work of evangelism. How do we do it? How can we influence others to Christ? There are three ways.

By Attitude

First, by our attitude. First Peter 3:15 says, "But sanctify the Lord God in your hearts, and always be ready to give a defense to everyone who asks you a reason for the hope that is within you." In other words, there should be such a radiance and joy and hope to our lives that others will ask about it, thus opening the door for us to share the gospel.

I'll never forget how this worked out once in my own experience. After I graduated from college I worked for a time at J. C. Penney's Department Store; and my supervisor was a young man who was not a Christian. I longed to witness to him, but the right occasion didn't seem to come. So I just did my work as well as I could and sought to maintain a good attitude. One day he came to me and said, "Robert, there's something different about you. You seem to have a sense of direction and hopefulness I've not seen before." That opened the door for

Katrina and me to invite him into our home where we were able to share Christ with him. I don't know what ever became of this young man and I cannot say that he actually became a Christian; but I felt the Lord had enabled us to plant a gospel seed in his heart. Our attitude of joy often precedes our words about Jesus.

By Action

We also witness by our acts. Matthew 5:16 says, "Let your light so shine before men, that they may see your good works and glorify your Father in heaven." Christianity is defined in the eyes of the world by the good works we do. Dr. Paul Maier, professor of ancient history at Western Michigan University, wrote the foreword to a book entitled *How Christianity Changed the World*, and he touched on this subject:

> Even knowledgeable believers will be amazed at how many of our present institutions and values reflect a Christian origin. Not only countless individual lives but civilization itself was transformed by Jesus Christ. In the ancient world, his teachings elevated brutish standards of morality, halted infanticide, enhanced human life, emancipated women, abolished slavery, inspired charities and relief organizations, created hospitals, established orphanages, and founded schools.
>
> In medieval times, Christianity almost singlehandedly kept classical culture alive through recopying manuscripts, building libraries, moderating warfare through truce days, and providing dispute

arbitration. It was Christians who invented colleges and universities, dignified labor as a divine vocation, and extended the light of civilization to barbarians on the frontiers.

In the modern era, Christian teaching, properly expressed, advanced science, instilled concepts of political and social and economic freedom, fostered justice, and provided the greatest single source of inspiration for the magnificent achievements in art, architecture, music, and literature that we treasure to this present day.... No other religion, philosophy, teaching, nation, movement—whatever—has so changed the world for the better as Christianity has done.[23]

Now, what is true on a historical perspective is also true on a personal level. The most powerful kind of witness we can bear are those good deeds and acts of kindness that communicate the love of Jesus Christ to another person. The Bible says, "They will know we are Christians by our love" (John 13:35).

By Assertiveness

Third, we witness by our assertiveness. While it's essential to witness by our attitudes and by our actions, sooner or later it's necessary for us to actually say a word for the Lord. We have to communicate the message of Christ by lip. It might be in the form of a simple sentence about Christ. It might be in a note or in a letter. It might be simply inviting someone to church or to an evangelistic event; but sooner or later we have to be assertive about our faith.

e = evangelism

Admittedly, this isn't very popular in our culture today, for it isn't considered "politically correct" to share our faith with unbelievers. But then, it's never been popular with the world when Christians share their faith. In the book of Acts, the Jewish Sanhedrin commanded those first apostles to shut up, to no longer preach in the name of Christ. "Don't evangelize," they said. "Don't tell others about your faith. Don't try to persuade someone else." But Peter and the apostles had two answers.

They said: "We must obey God rather than men" (Acts 5:29, NIV).

They also said: "We cannot possibly keep quiet. Whether it is right in the sight of God to listen to you more than to God, you judge. But we cannot help but speak the things which we have seen and heard" (Acts 4:19, 20, my paraphrase).

I'll admit that I'm seldom comfortable when I open my mouth to witness for Christ. Even after years of working on it, I'm shy and nervous as a rule. But I've learned that our greatest earthly joy is leading someone else to Christ. When I gave my life fully to Christ as a sophomore in college, I developed a burden to share Christ with others. A friend encouraged me to go with him to a local mall and witness. I kept a record of those who made decisions for Christ, and just the other week I came across those names:

- 1-30-1972: Randy Brown (about 20)
- 2-4-1972: Charles Buckner (about 16)
- 2-4-1972: Gerry Gyton (about 13)
- 2-4-1972: Jimmy Bickly (about 15)
- 2-6-1972: Kevin Weekley (about 16)

Simple

- 4-15-1972: Ray Landrey (soldier at Fort Jackson)
- 4-15-1972: James Lee (soldier at Fort Jackson, Mormon background)

I don't know what became of any of these people; I hope some of them were truly saved and have continued with the Lord. But the memory of those days is very precious, and I can say that the greatest experiences I've had as a pastor are those times when we have seen people embracing Christ as Savior and Lord.

Recently while we were traveling in Israel, a young man in our group asked me if he could be baptized in the Jordan River. "Yes," I replied, "can you tell me when you received Christ into your heart?" To my surprise, he told me he had prayed to receive Christ at our church's Easter Service at the Grand Ole Opry House two years ago.

I had preached on the Resurrection of Christ, and at the end of the message I had led people in praying the "sinner's prayer" for salvation. He had quietly joined in that prayer, but he had not communicated that to me until now. Had we not been traveling together, I'm not sure I would have known of it.

When you invite someone to church, take them to a gospel service, or say a word for the Lord, you never know how God may use that in another person's life. Only in heaven will we see the full measure of our work for the Lord. But there comes a time when we have to be assertive in sharing our faith, for the love of Christ compels us to do so.

Several years ago, someone gave me a little book entitled *Jungle Harvest*, written by missionary Ruby Scott about her experiences among the Tila Indians in the jungles of south Mexico. Ruby and her colleague translated the message of the Bible into the Tila language; and they arranged to have the gospel recorded and duplicated on records that could be played on small crank-operated record players.

One of the men who heard the message was a witch doctor named Domingo. He was in his mid-fifties and illiterate, and his face was a sea of wrinkles. Domingo turned from his old way of life and was wonderfully converted. He instantly became burdened for his old friends, the other witch doctors in his former village. One day he decided to take the message to them. He borrowed one of the portable record players and the records (which the Tilas called Talking Black Tortillas), and off he went.

His former friends were happy to see him, and they talked, laughed, and reminisced about the old days. When Domingo opened up the record player, they watched him with great curiosity and began listening. After playing some of the Scriptures, Domingo told them that God had turned his heart around. He shared his own testimony with them and preached the gospel to them.

They responded angrily, "How can you, who have experienced the power and authority of a witch doctor, turn your back on the very gods who have chosen you?" They argued and threatened him. Domingo remained calm and kept preaching Jesus to them. Finally, his friends grabbed their machetes and ordered him to leave.

Domingo hastily closed the phonograph and slipped the records into his carrying bag. Swinging the machine onto his back, he turned sadly and started down the trail. But his heart was heavy and he felt he had to make one more try. Turning back, he began to say another word for Christ.

In anger, one of the men raised his machete and aimed it at Domingo's phonograph. Domingo's hand touched the machine to steady it, and the machete sliced off three fingers. Domingo hurried away, and when he was out of sight tore a sleeve from his shirt to bandage his bleeding hand. Then he trudged home.

Two days later, as Ruby Scott was dressing the stumps of his fingers, she coaxed him to tell her exactly what had happened. He told the story, then after a long pause, he looked at her and said, "Those poor men! God's message just didn't grab their hearts. I'll go back and tell them again."

In her book, Ruby wrote that she stayed awake a long time that night, staring into the dark and thinking of Domingo's crippled hand and of his quiet words, "I'll go back and tell them again."

She thought of the times she had failed to witness to her friends, the times she had grown discouraged with her witnessing, and the times she had failed to go back and tell them again.

"I turned over," she said, "struggled to my knees in the cramped confines under my mosquito net, and rededicated my life to the Lord. I asked Him to make me as faithful a missionary as this humble, illiterate former witch doctor."[24]

Sometimes we have to keep telling them again and again. That doesn't mean we have to be great preachers or world famous evangelists. An evangelist is one who shares the Good News of Christ whether the audience is a great multitude in a stadium or one child sitting on our patio.

e = evangelism

When we think of modern-day evangelists we think of men like Billy Graham, but let me tell you about another evangelist who used a different method—Billy's wife, Ruth. Years ago, when Mr. Graham was conducting a month long crusade in London, there was a girl named Wendy who came to the meetings. She was heavily involved in drugs, and somehow Ruth met her and the two began talking. One evening before the service began, Ruth said, "One day you will come to something difficult in your life. And then you will either go back on drugs or go on with Christ."

A few days before the end of the crusade, as Ruth was sitting in her seat at Earls Court she was handed a note. It was from Wendy, and it simply said, "I am on drugs. Come help me." Ruth found Wendy almost unconscious by the stadium entrance. A friend explained that Wendy's best friend had died from an overdose that afternoon. Ruth searched through her pocket for something to write on and found a little box of tissue. Using the cardboard backing she wrote, "God loves me. Jesus died for me. No matter what I've done, if

If you cannot preach like Peter,
if you cannot pray like Paul,
You can tell the love of Jesus,
and say He died for all.

I confess to Him, He will forgive me." She tucked the cardboard into Wendy's pocket and asked one of the crusade staff to drive Wendy home.

A year passed, and the two women met again. Wendy had no recollection of asking Ruth for help and she had no idea how that note had come to be in her pocket. But she said it was the lifeline that brought her to Jesus Christ.

Simple

While her husband was preaching to thousands of people and reaching the great multitudes, Ruth was stuffing a little gospel note into the pocket of just one person; but that note made all the difference.[25]

This story reminds me of something Lorne Sanny said in his little book on personal evangelism.

> "We may not be like Peter who preached one day and 3000 were added to the church. We can be like Andrew, however, who after he had been brought to the Savior, found his brother, Peter, and brought him to the Lord Jesus. Peter fished with a net, so to speak, and caught large numbers. Andrew fished with a pole and line, catching one fish at a time. We may not be called upon to preach to great multitudes or even to groups, yet we can witness effectively to individuals one by one—the pole and line method. What a privilege that can be! We, like Andrew, might lead someone to the Lord, and that one, in turn, might lead thousands."[26]

Where can you begin? Who needs to see Jesus in you?

Simple Memory:
"But sanctify the Lord God in your hearts, and always be ready to give a defense to everyone who asks you a reason for the hope that is in you, with meekness and fear" (I Peter 3:5).

Notes

1. Taken from *How to Be Sure You Are a Christian*. Copyright © 1972 by Bill Bright. Published by NewLife Publications, Orlando, FL. Used by permission. All rights reserved.
2. R. A. Torrey, *How to Succeed in the Christian Life* (Chicago: Moody Press, u.d.), p 23. Used by permission.
3. Taken from *Explore the Book—VOL V* by J. Sidlow Baxter. Copyright © J. Sidlow Baxter. Used by permission of The Zondervan Corporation.
4. Adapted from the author's book *He Shall Be Called*, published by Warner Faith Press, 2005.
5. For portions of this imagery, I am indebted to Willard M. Aldrich in his article entitled "Assurance" in *Bibliotheca Sacra*: A quarterly published by Dallas Theological Seminary. Jul-Sept. 1957, vol. 114.
6. Adapted from George Sweeting, *How to Begin the Christian Life* (Chicago: Moody Press, 1970), p. 106. Sweeting's version is a close rendering to a similar passage in R. A. Torrey's *How To Succeed in the Christian Life* (Chicago: Moody Press, u.d.), p. 24. Used by permission.
7. A type is any person, event, or object in the Old Testament that prefigures or predicts some aspect of Jesus Christ as seen in the New Testament.
8. Taken from *Baptism* © Copyright 2000 by Larry E. Dyer. Published by Kregel Publications, Grand Rapids, MI. Used by permission of the publisher. All rights reserved.
9. *Marcartney's Illustrations*. Used by permission of the American Tract Society, Garland, Texas.
10. Source unknown.
11. Vance Havner, *In Times Like These* (Old Tappan, NJ: Fleming H. Revell Co., 1969), p. 73.
12. Source unknown.
13. Isobel Kuhn, *In the Arena* (Singapore: OMF Books, 1995), pp. 30-32.
14. Bertha Smith, *Go Home and Tell* (Nashville: Broadman & Holman Publishers, 1995), p. 76.
15. Thomas Watson, *Gleanings From Thomas Watson* (Morgan, PA: Soli Deo Gloria Publications [Ligonier Ministries], 1995, first published in London in 1915), p. 107.
16. Iris Clinton, *Young Man in a Hurry: The Story of William Carey* (Fort Washington, PA: Christian Literature Crusade, 1961), pp. 55, 56.
17. R. A. Torrey, *How to Succeed in the Christian Life* (Chicago: Moody Press, u.d.), p. 50. Permission granted.

Notes

18. A. P. Fitt, *The Life of D. L. Moody* (Chicago: Moody Press, u.d.), p. 114. Used by permission.

19. Jill Morgan, *A Man of the Word: Life of G. Campbell Morgan* (Grand Rapids: Baker Book House, 1972), p. 342.

20. John C. Polluck, *A Foreign Devil in China* (Minneapolis, Minnesota: World Publications, 1971), p. 52.

21. Source unknown.

22. Lorne Sanny, *The Art of Personal Witnessing* (Chicago: Moody Press, 1957), p. 9. Used by permission.

23. Taken from *How Christianity Changed the World* by Alvin J. Schmidt. Copyright © 2001, 2004 by Alvin J. Schmidt. Used by permission of The Zondervan Corporation.

24. Ruby Scott, *Jungle Harvest* (privately published by Ruby Scott and the Conservative Baptist Home Mission Society, 1988), pp. 45-48.

25. "Wendy's Story" by Julie Nixon Eisenhower in *Ruth Graham: Celebrating an Extraordinary Life*, complied by Stephen Griffith (Nashville: W Publishing, 2003) pp. 116, 117.

26. Lorne Sanny, *The Art of Personal Witnessing* (Chicago: Moody Press, 1957), pp. 8, 9. Used by permission.

Robert J. Morgan is a best-selling and Gold-Medallion winning writer with well over a million books in print. He is the pastor of the Donelson Fellowship in Nashville, Tennessee, where he has served for 25 years. He and his wife Katrina have three daughters and five grandchildren.

Interested in Sharing

Simple?

Churches, organizations, and individuals ordering by case can purchase *Simple* at $4.99 each. Twenty-four copies per case. Call to order: 1-800-877-7030

group or individual studies from Randall House

Regaining Balance:
91 Days of Prayer and Praise
Randy Sawyer

Regaining Balance is a devotional journal designed to guide its readers through a season of spiritual revival. A free, on-line Leader's Guide (www.RandallHouse.com) allows pastors and Bible study leaders to utilize this devotional in a group setting.
ISBN 0892655186
$9.99

Bulk Discounts available. Call 1-800-877-7030 for more information.

THROUGH THE EYES OF GOD
John Marshall

This story and study are based upon Dr. Marshall's own journey from spectator to active player in the arena of missions. *Through the Eyes of God* inspires and encourages pastors and laypeople alike to be obedient to the Great Commission. Free, on-line Leader's Guide at www.RandallHouse.com. Discussion/Study Questions Included
ISBN 0892655135
$9.99